Joyosity
Works
Playbook

JOYOSITYWORKS
MEDIA
Saint Louis, Missouri

Joyosity Works Media | www.joyosityworksmedia.com

All trademarks are the property of their respective companies.

Cover Design: Catherine Casalino
Author photo: Jeff Brown
Interior Design: Jessica Angerstein

ISBN: 979-8-9937525-0-1

1 2 3 4 5 6 7 8 9 10

Joyosity Works Playbook

Practical Plays + Strategies for Joy at Work + Beyond

THE OFFICIAL COMPANION TO
*JOYOSITY: HOW TO CULTIVATE INTENSE HAPPINESS
IN WORK & LIFE (EVEN IF THINGS ARE WHAT THEY ARE)*

Jenn Whitmer

JOYOSITYWORKS
MEDIA

Contents

The Playbook to Restore Joy

Arms crossed and slumped in plastic chairs, the team meeting focused on the huge challenge before them.

They're heading into a must-win match against the best team in the league. If they lost, they'd be relegated—facing transfers, pay cuts, and a hard hit to their pride. After a season of stellar losses, it's clear that business as usual won't save them. They need new plays.

The coaches—black marker in hand at the whiteboard—asked the team for every off-the-wall, seemingly unhinged plays they've ever tried. Players started shouting out names like *Pepper Shakers*, *Midnight Poutine*, *Upside-Town Taxi*, and *Loki's Toboggan*. This isn't *Switching the Field* or the *One-Two*. These plays are designed to shake up the game.

And that's where you are now.

You've run done the work of work—the strategies, drills, and habits the productivity and profit idols have written. That old workbook may have taken you a ways, but at what cost? Exhaustion, anxiety, and the constant question: *Is this worth it?*

You're holding this Playbook because you know it's time for a new way—plays with creativity, connection, and curiosity that cultivate joy. When you first try some of these plays, their simplicity may surprise you. You may feel a touch of concern—is this even allowed? You might even question whether you are capable of building a life of joy.

The truth is: Joy is what will save you. And you're ready to cultivate it.

You'll get the most from this *Playbook* if you've read *Joyosity: How to Cultivate Intense Happiness in Work and Life (Even If Things Are What They Are)*. That book fully explored the big concepts, data, research, and neuroscience behind these plays. First, let's do a quick review of our current joy problem and how Joyosity works to solve it.

Where we are in the game: We are literally dying without joy. Leaders worldwide are experiencing a surge in burnout, disengagement, and toxic work cultures.

Five roadblocks to joy: You face 5 main opponents in cultivating a life of joy.

1. *Obsession with measurement:* "If you can't measure it, you can't manage it," is the harmful myth which ignores that metrics, while important, are insufficient.

2. *Tradition:* The fallacy "This is how we've always done it" disregards that we have radically changed how, when, and where we work.

3. *It's not that bad:* We've normalized dysfunctional and toxic environments—gaslighting, blame shifting, and boundary violations—perpetuating the cycle of stress and harm.

4. *Work before play:* From childhood homework to PTO accrual, we operate like rest must be earned. This overemphasis on productivity creates a culture where rest and joy are considered luxuries rather than necessities for being a human.

5. *We're not worthy:* Most of us don't believe we deserve joy. Yet joy is precisely what fuels sustainability, adaptability, and resilience.

Joy creates success: Joy is intense happiness rooted in deep connection and appreciation, experiencing something bigger than yourself. Joyful employees significantly boost productivity, collaboration, and overall profitability. Joy is not a feel-good extra but a legitimate driver of overall success, health, and well-being.

Run the plays for joy: You're holding your playbook to cultivate joy. You'll find practical tactics, exercises, and strategies to help you lead, work, and live with real joy. These plays take theory and put it smack into the middle of your day.

Information
ain't
transformation.

How to Use this Book

We're following the Joyosity Compass—the same structure from *Joyosity*. Each section helps you explore your self, engage with others, and experience joy in your real life.

Chapter Highlights

- **Chapter 1**: Revisit the Joy Ratio and use the Joyosity Explorer Map to define joy in your playing field—what Joyosity looks like for you
- **Chapter 2**: Name your patterns with the Johari Window and the Enneagram personality framework with 3 plays that build joy and strength for your type

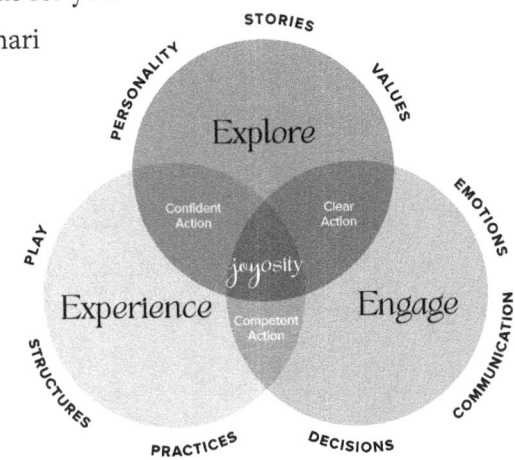

- **Chapter 3**: Write new plays for your mental game. Combine self-efficacy and the Enneagram to shift your inner script and transform your leadership
- **Chapter 4**: Complete the NAVIGATE process to identify, define, and operationalize your values
- **Chapter 5**: Practice emotional intelligence skills with the Enneagram Feels Wheel
- **Chapter 6**: Build on the CLEAN framework of communication. Incorporate curiosity, stories, and nonverbal congruence to communicate effectively
- **Chapter 7**: Strengthen your conflict skills. Identify strategies for each Enneagram type, universal tactics for healthy conflict, and the four stages of repair
- **Chapter 8**: Build your Personal Board, practice being a Wanter, and add other tools to the Decision Insight Decoder for wise decision-making

- **Chapter 9**: Identify practices that fuel your joy—breathwork, social connection, and more—so you're leading from overflow, not fumes
- **Chapter 10**: Design and evaluate structures that fit the person you are now. Integrate systems, rhythms, and rituals in your Designed Week so you build productivity on joy, not hustle
- **Chapter 11**: Put play to work in your career and problem-solving. Use play tactics to hone your craft, get unstuck, and innovate—your own *Loki's Toboggan*
- **Play It Forward**: Evaluate a pattern to revisit these ideas so you don't stop at a little fun but design a life of joy
- **Appendix A**: Full Enneagram type descriptions as a resource for yourself and others
- **Appendix B**: Fillable frameworks to use again and again. Visit the online resources to print more and access interactive tools.

Where to Begin

You like order: Start at the beginning! You'll play a great game following the linear order of Explore, Engage, and Experience.

You know the play you need: Jump right in. Many of the frameworks overlap, so start where you want and add as you go.

You need help: If it all feels important or you just don't know what you need the most, watch the "Clarity Over Chaos" workshop (access in Appendix B). I'll guide you through an audit exercise with the Joyosity Compass, so you begin where it matters most.

Your Playbook on the Field

I designed this *Playbook* for you to write in, highlight, and carry into meetings, not left pristine on a shelf. I highly recommend handwriting as much as possible.

When you see this icon ⏱ *20 minutes* that's your estimated focus time for the exercise. If it's under 20 minutes, go for completing it in one sitting. For longer exercises, I'll mark natural stages.

When you see **The Extra Mile:** that's your cue to go deeper or extend the application when you're ready.

Write all over these pages. Add the date when you start an exercise so you can see your growth. When you want to use the plays again, grab the fillable frameworks from Appendix B.

You've got the ballpoint pen. Let's play for joy.

Whistle!

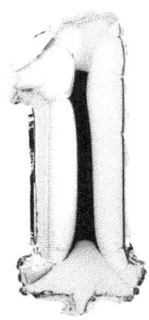

Map Your Joy Game

In the first chapters of *Joyosity*, we discussed how leaders aren't merely drowning in stress; they're dying from it. This isn't sustainable, and the research shows the way we're doing work doesn't work.

You don't have to live this way. To bring joy into work and all of your life, you need to reject sterile, profit-and-productivity blocks to joy and create success with the Joy Ratio: Joy's Magic Third, Toil's Tiny Ten, and the Messy Middle.

You can't identify whether you're in the Joy Ratio if you don't know what brings you joy or what drains it. That's the starting line.

Joyosity Explorer Map

As you go through the map, don't filter or edit, just write.

Stop 1: Joy-Givers

Joy's Magic Third

Look for the markers of the deep roots of joy:

1. You feel lucky, favored, or fortunate to do the work.
2. You feel connected because of your work. You feel a sense of belonging.
3. The work has purpose. It impacts other people.

What activities, people, and experiences bring you joy and energy? What brings you life when you're doing it and remains when it's over? Be specific. No idea is too small.

Joy-Givers | Date:

Your goal is to have these activities make up 35% of your time.

Stop 2: Joy-Drainers

Toil's Tiny Ten

Toil is the opposite of joy. We're trying to keep it under 10% of your time. This includes:

1. The work that drains you.
2. The work that feels meaningless.
3. The work doesn't interest you, or you don't have the skills and resources to enjoy it.

What activities, people, and experiences drain your joy and energy? What do you dread, feel exhausted or overextended when you're doing it and leaves you feeling weary when it's over? Again, be specific. Nothing is too small.

Joy-Drainers | Toil:

Stop 3: Exploration

Expand a little more from the lists above. Use the prompts below to explore the reasons your lists bring you joy or drain it.

What do you love about to do? What about that activity brings you joy? How do you feel after?

_____

_____

_____

What do you avoid doing? What are the reasons you avoid it?

_____

_____

_____

If you could spend 1/3 of your day doing the work activity that brings you the most joy, what would be on that list?

_____

_____

_____

Who is helped by your work? What problem do you solve with or for them?

_____

_____

_____

If you could stop any activities, what would you stop doing?

_____

_____

_____

If you could wave a magic wand, what would you change about your work?

_____

_____

_____

What are the reasons you took this role or chose this career?

_____

_____

_____

Stop 4: Make Choices

With your answers from Stop 3, make choices about what to keep doing and what to stop.

What are you already doing that you want to keep doing or want to do more of? What brings you the most joy? Choose 6-8.

_____

_____

_____

_____

What from your list above would devastate you if you had to stop it? Choose 3-4 items from your list above.

_____

_____

_____

_____

What toil from your joy-draining and toil list would you like to stop or move away from? Choose 3-4.

_____

_____

_____

_____

What from the toil list above would you walk away from today and never look back? Chose 1-2.

_____

_____

_____

_____

Stop 5: Take Action

Making a choice isn't enough. You have to act. And often, clarity is in the action. The next step isn't final. It's a trial or beginning.

Choose 1 thing from the joy-giving list from Stop 4 that you want to do more of or make sure you do daily. Choose the 1 that feels the most exciting or the easiest to maintain.

I'll build my joy by: _____

_____

Choose 1 thing from the joy-draining list in Map Stop 4 that you want to stop doing of or do less of every day. Again, choose the 1 that feels the most freeing if you stopped it or the easiest to do less of it.

Let's see what happens when I stop: _____

Choose when you're starting. Today? Next Tuesday? Set a start date.

I will start on: _____

_____

Now put it in your calendar. (Yes, open your calendar and make an appointment.)

Saying it out loud makes it real and puts some positive accountability in place. Share your action with a trusted friend or colleague or me. I'd love to cheer you on!

The Extra Mile: Check Your Math

For 1 week, pause midday, the end of the workday, and before bed to review how you've spent your time. Estimate how many minutes you spent in joy, toil, or the messy middle.

Day 1	Day 2	Day 3	Day 4	Day 5	Day 6	Day 7
Morning						
Joy:	Joy:	Joy:	Joy:	Joy:	Joy:	Joy:
Toil:	Toil:	Toil:	Toil:	Toil:	Toil:	Toil:
Middle:	Middle:	Middle:	Middle:	Middle:	Middle:	Middle:
Afternoon						
Joy:	Joy:	Joy:	Joy:	Joy:	Joy:	Joy:
Toil:	Toil:	Toil:	Toil:	Toil:	Toil:	Toil:
Middle:	Middle:	Middle:	Middle:	Middle:	Middle:	Middle:
Evening						
Joy:	Joy:	Joy:	Joy:	Joy:	Joy:	Joy:
Toil:	Toil:	Toil:	Toil:	Toil:	Toil:	Toil:
Middle:	Middle:	Middle:	Middle:	Middle:	Middle:	Middle:

Find your percentage in each category.

Category minutes ÷ total minutes = percent of time

For example, if joy time is 1,638 minutes and the total time is 6,300 minutes.

$$1,638 \div 6,300 = 0.26 = 26\%$$

Repeat for each category time to see your current time ratio.

Knowing what brings you joy and what is toil provides the clarity you need to design your life around real joy. Sometimes you need a little more help. You can always hop on a call with me at jennwhitmer.com/spark-call. Sometimes it's just easier to talk it out.

To have joy, stop settling for a lesser, dishonest version of yourself.

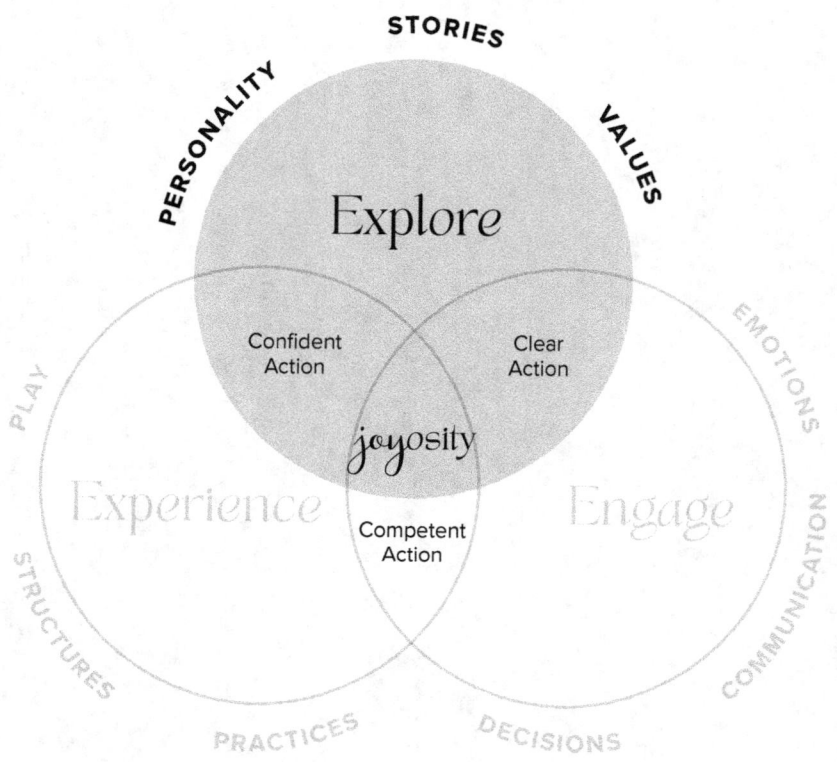

Part One

Explore

Who's on the Field

Leadership requires ruthless self-honesty and radical self-compassion. Curiosity balances you on this tightrope.

The plays in the Explore section will help you grow in understanding yourself through your personality, mindset, and values.

These are the plays to becoming your favorite self and living a life of joy.

Know Your Patterns of Play

Self-awareness is where the roots of joy begin.

Without understanding yourself, every play at growth is guesswork. Understanding yourself helps you choose the right tactics as a leader but also gives you more choices that are honest and freeing—even when you feel like you're winging it.

In this chapter, you'll use two powerful frameworks to deepen awareness: the Johari Window, which shows you the four areas of self-awareness so you can change, and the Enneagram, which shows you *why* you think, act, and feel the way you do. Together, they give you a clear view of your patterns and the practical steps to grow joy from the inside out.

Using Johari

The Johari Window illustrates the four areas of self-awareness. Each quadrant holds different information that you need to holistically understand yourself. If a section is missing, your joy isn't rooted in reality.

Johari Window

	Known to Self	Hidden from Self
Known to Others	Open	Blind Spot
Hidden from Others	Façade	Unknown

Johari Window

OPEN: Where you can make choices for growth toward joy.

FAÇADE: The way from Façade to Open is self-disclosure.

BLIND SPOT: The way from Blind Spot to Open is feedback.

UNKNOWN: The way from Unknown to Blind Spot or Façade is naming patterns, motivations, and triggers.

Interactive Window

Let's put the Johari window to work for you. Start with the Johari window with questions here. Appendix B has a blank one for making copies, or you can draw your own.

These questions here are for personal and professional development. You can also use them for workloads, project transfers, and more. When answering these questions, remember to balance ruthless self-honesty and radical self-compassion by engaging curiosity.

	Known to Self	Hidden from Self
Known to Others	**OPEN** Questions that you and at least 1 other person answer the same. 1. What professional or personal practice am I currently working on? 2. Who knows or who needs to know? 3. What is my action step or practice? 4. When does this action step happen? Is it on the calendar?	**BLIND SPOT** Ask people you trust to be honest, kind, and specific. You can also narrow to an area you want to work on such as follow-through or communication. 1. What is 1 observable behavior that causes friction or holds me back? 2. What is 1 observable behavior that is a clear strength and benefits me and/or the group?
Hidden from Others	**FAÇADE** These are personal reflection questions. You decide the method of disclosure. 1. What perceptions do I hear from others that surprise me? 2. When do I assume people know what I mean or how I feel? 3. Are there skills, goals, values, or passions I haven't shared with others that could help collaboration or relationships? 4. What do I need to disclose to others? Specifically to whom?	**UNKNOWN** These reflection questions uncover what's hidden. 1. What actions or words will activate or upset me? 2. When do I get defensive? 3. When do I notice my Enneagram personality Fundamental Fear or Persistent Pattern show up? 4. When do I get most excited? 5. What repeatedly puzzles me?

Enneagram Personality Types

In my house, everything has a home. And I like to say to myself and to the rest of my family, "Everything has a home, and everything in its home." And people tell me all the time, "You're so organized!"

I don't feel organized. The reason everything has a home is because I can't remember where I put stuff unless it's always in the same place. If I dig a little bit deeper, it feels painful to waste time because that feels like missing out, and that is all about the Enneagram Seven motivation of avoiding pain. It's not the outward action of organization that shows my personality type; it's the deeper motivation of *why* I'm organized.

The Enneagram personality framework shows why you feel, think, and act the way you do. It's not about the outward behaviors—it's always about the deeper motivations. Bring what you learned from *Joyosity* and use this section of the *Playbook* to solidify and learn more about your type. Below are short descriptions and a list of what it's like to be that type. Appendix A has longer descriptions for you.

Remember, this information uses patterns and defaults as a way for you to understand yourself and others better. You won't identify with every single part of your type structure. You're finding the one the describes you the best overall—the one that makes you feel a little squeamish and a bit consoled. Tests, checklists, and descriptions are simply guides. Only you can decide what your true motivations are. If you want more guidance, an Enneagram Navigator session is for you.

After the description of each type are 3 paths toward joy for that type. Use these to apply this knowledge so it produces joy.

Here are the commitments you're making in using the Enneagram to create more joy:

1. Curiosity is the foundation. When you experience discomfort, channel curiosity.
2. Start with yourself. It's easy to avoid what feels tender by focusing on other people. Figure yourself out first.
3. No swords or shields. Use the Enneagram to build up, encourage, and grow in joy. Period.

Body Group: Eights, Nines, Ones

Primary Emotional Struggle: Anger and Control
Deepest Desires: Justice, Respect, Belonging

Eight: The Protective Challenger

Eights believe they have to be strong because it's not safe to trust anyone. They use denial (refusing to acknowledge their vulnerability or limits) to avoid feeling weak or betrayed, and to maintain a self-image of being powerful and in control. Eights want belonging, but they'll settle for power.

If You're an **Enneagram Eight,** You'll Get This

- I've been told I'm intimidating or aggressive.
- Doing things halfway is not my thing.
- My BS detector is military-grade.
- Overly nice people make me suspicious.
- Being direct cuts through the noise.
- I don't look for conflict, but I'm not running from it.
- My gut makes decisions while some people are still trying to understand the problem.
- I give zero Fs what you think of me.

- Beneath the armor, I'm scared to be controlled.
- Trust takes time. Earn it, and you'll have me for life. Break it, and you're gone for good.
- If I trust you, I'll happily take a break from being in charge.
- When I walk into a room, I know who holds the power.
- Justice is always worth fighting for.
- What people don't realize is that I have a giant heart.
- I know people respect me, but knowing I belong would be amazing.

Three Shifts That Build Joy and Strength for Enneagram Eights

1. **Vulnerability will crack you open to joy.** (Please keep the book open!) The Genie Pass to growth is being 100% honest about your emotions, fears, hurts, and even wounds from long ago.

    I'm sure, "Oh, hell no," just jumped into your mind. But if you want to grow, this is the way. Start small and use your strength to move beyond your fear. You're going to practice with trusted people.

    Let's start that list. Write 5 people you could imagine exploring this with:

    _____

    _____

    _____

    _____

2. **You're not indestructible. And that's really ok.** Your vast capacity and intensity won't protect you from your very human limits. When you're always pushing past your actual resources, you will break things you don't anticipate like bones, relationships, and communities. That will leave you in the very place you're trying to avoid—completely dependent on someone else.

    Where are you pushing the limits of your body, time, relationships, or money?

Body	Time
Relationships	Money

    Where are you going at it 110%, trying to prove your strength or power? Could you pull back to 80%? You don't have to do all 4, but pick 1: _____

3. **Truth without kindness is cruel.** (And not because people can't handle it.) Sometimes you believe you hold the deed to truth. In reality, other people are perfectly within their rights to have a different perspective and even a different version of truth. Grey has many shades. Black and white aren't the only options. When you bust forward (often uninvited) with brutal truths, you can damage work, relationships, and even cause trauma.

   Before you "say it like it is," pause and consider:

   1. What if I'm wrong? (I know, but it is possible.)
   2. What am I not seeing?
   3. What is my intention? Care and love or power and vindication?

One more thing: When you take off the armor, joy can finally get close.

Nine: The Harmonious Peacemaker

Nines believe they have to be harmonious and comfortable because it's not ok to assert themselves. They use narcotization (numbing out) to avoid conflict and to maintain a self-image of being comfortable or harmonious. Nines want to be connected, but they'll settle for keeping the peace.

If You're an **Enneagram Nine,** You'll Get This

+ I value harmony more than being right.
+ I'm easy to be around—people tell me I'm a safe place to land.
+ I can see every side of an issue.
+ "I'm fine with whatever" is my default. And yes, people wish I were more engaged.
+ I'll do almost anything to avoid conflict.
+ I'm quietly stubborn when people push me.
+ I'm good at escaping demands by drifting away.
+ I don't always know what I want, but I can tell you what everyone else needs.

+ I'm a pro-procrastinator. I get lost in little tasks while the big thing waits.
+ Getting started is hard, but once I do, I really get things done.
+ Home, naps, comfort TV, and cozy blankets are my love language. I am hygge.
+ Anger feels dangerous to relationships, so I try to forget it.
+ People see me as peaceful; sometimes I'm just checked out.
+ Sometimes I surprise people. They think it was a bold move, but it doesn't feel out of character to me.
+ I want to know I matter enough to speak my truth and act on it.

Three Shifts That Build Joy and Strength for Enneagram Nines

1. **Stop the knee jerk "yes."** Your desire to be easygoing so you avoid discomfort and disconnection distances you from what you want. This habit also keeps you over-extended. Lots of words around Nines just aren't true. You're not slothful or lazy; you've disconnected from yourself and spend too much mental energy keeping the peace.

   Two ways to practice this skill. Start with the easier 1:

   • *"Let me think about it."* Practice responding to a request with that phrase. Then you have time to consider if you actually want to do it. If you do, great! But if you're not sure or don't want to, you can respond with a little space.

- *"That doesn't work for me."* No is a fine response, but this phrase also lets you practice saying "for me" and standing on your own wants.

These feel challenging. But when you don't stand as your own person, you not only miss out on your own joy, you also keep the rest of us from experiencing the greatness that you have to offer.

2. **Explore the Magic Zone by practicing discomfort.**
Your Nine personality is telling you discomfort means belonging is gone. But so much of life is moving through discomfort. Conflicts will happen. Change will happen. Mistakes will happen. Learning new things will happen. And all of them require discomfort. You need to know you will be okay even if you're experiencing discomfort.

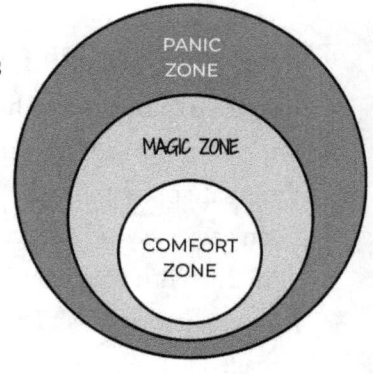

Pick a "hard" thing to do once a week. Physically is a great place to start, but it can also be emotionally. Choose a way to expand just beyond what feels comfortable and what you think you're capable of.

Build a streak and reward yourself at the end with something you want to do. Start with 12 weeks. Write what you did and check it off!

Reward:	

3. **Big loud purpose.** Systems, rhythms, and rituals will help you reduce decision fatigue (remember chapter 11 of *Joyosity*?). For Nines, deciding what you do first, second, and so on can trip you up every day. You need a filter that helps you decide what matters most. And that's your purpose.

Review your purpose statement from chapter 4. Write it here:

_____

_____

_____

_____

_____

_____

Now write it on a note card. Put the card up where you can see it.

Start your day by reading your statement (Yes, with your out loud voice!). When you then look at what you want to do each day, you can see if it connects to your purpose. Ask yourself: _Does this help me accomplish my purpose?_ You can do this with goals and big projects as well.

The Extra Mile: set a reminder in your phone for a time during the day when your purpose will pop up.

One more thing: You don't risk connection when you engage. You invite joy.

One: The Reforming Perfectionist

Ones believe they have to be right to be good because it's not ok to make mistakes. They use reaction formation (acting out the opposite of genuine feelings) and masking to avoid anger and to maintain a self-image of being right. Ones want to be good, but they'll settle for being right.

If You're an **Enneagram One,** You'll Get This

- ✦ I'm a champion of what's good and right (even when it's exhausting).
- ✦ Most of my life, I've believed that if I do the right thing, things will be good.
- ✦ I organized the fun. You're welcome.
- ✦ It's almost ready... not quite right yet... just this little tweak. I'm nothing if not thorough.
- ✦ I can find every typo, crooked frame, and unfinished corner.
- ✦ Perfect isn't easy. It's rare and hard—but worth it.
- ✦ I could really be better at... well, everything. And yes, you could be better at a few things, too.
- ✦ If I don't actively rein in my emotions and impulses, I might say or do something inappropriate and feel ashamed.

- ✦ I don't always know what's "good enough" to move on.
- ✦ If I do it right, I'll avoid criticism and failure.
- ✦ If I do everything by the book, then if something goes wrong, it can't be my fault.
- ✦ Everybody thinks I need to be right; I just want to make sure we're following the rules.
- ✦ I didn't realize other people don't have a voice in their head saying, "You're doing it wrong."
- ✦ I can't rest until the work is done... and sometimes not even then.
- ✦ Beneath it all, I just want to know I'm good enough to belong as I am.

Three Shifts That Build Joy and Strength for Enneagram Ones

1. **Put the inner critic in its place.** Your inner critic isn't kind or helpful, and most of the time, it's lying to you. The critic has become how you measure your own goodness and success. You're so used to trusting and obeying this voice, you have to untangle from it so you can practice self-compassion.

Give your critic a name. With my clients who are Ones, the most effective is an off-the-wall name and identity. This diminishes its power and helps you frame the voice for what it often is: ridiculous. (If you're a Harry Potter fan, basically your inner critic is a boggart. This is the Riddikulus charm effect.) You can't do this wrong. And you can change it later if you want.

Brainstorm your name list here.

Now draw it or list characteristics of this persona (age, style, gender...).

Now when your inner critic stands up, say this: "Thanks, _____, for your input and trying to keep me from mistakes. You can sit down now."

2. **Get comfortable with GETMO.** Perfect is a myth. You will rob yourself (and others) from so much joy if you keep trying to make it perfect. Mistakes are part of being human, and your incredibly high standards sometimes keep you from doing all the great work you want to do. The saying "Done is better than perfect," from Anne Mollegen Smith is true, but it doesn't give you a lot to go on as a One. Because to you, it's not done until it's perfect.

   Enter GETMO: Good Enough to Move On. This concept from Craig Groeschel is getting to the sweet spot of effort and impact. Perfection is a bottomless pit of despair. You can tweak, nudge, adjust, and edit for-literal-ever. And in that process, you will exhaust yourself, frustrate your collaborators, and never finish anything.

   When you find yourself opening the deck again to nudge the text box, staying up to make just a few changes to your data charts, or procrastinating, ask yourself:
   - Is this worth my energy?
   - What am I sacrificing to make this "perfect"?
   - Am I taking away someone else's learning opportunity?
   - What does good enough look like?

   And when your inner bogart starts shouting at you, see number 1 above!

3. **Move rest and play up on your list.** Rest is a practice not a prize. If you are waiting to earn rest when all the work is done, you will slowly destroy your body and your spirit. When Ones put off rest, fun, and delight, resentment skyrockets. "Everyone else gets to relax, but I don't." Friend, you are the one keeping you from the fun.

   Rest and play are biological imperatives. So you will find a way to "sneak pleasure," which causes a cycle of shame, over-functioning, self-punishment, and more resentment. Incorporate moments of play and rest every day. Schedule it and put it on your to-do list.

List a dozen activities that are fun or restful to you.

1.	7.
2.	8.
3.	9.
4.	10.
5.	11.
6.	12.

One more thing: When you shush the critic, you can hear joy's voice.

Heart Group: Twos, Threes, Fours

Primary Emotional Struggle: Shame & Guilt
Deepest Desires: Significance, Identity, Validation, and Love

Two: The Considerate Giver

Twos believe they have to be helpful because it's not ok to have their own needs. They use repression of personal needs and feelings to avoid being needy and to maintain a self-image of being helpful. Twos want love, but they'll settle for appreciation.

If You're an **Enneagram Two,** You'll Get This

- I've heard the life story of at least 12 strangers at Target.
- "Are you thirsty? Did you eat yet?" are my constant questions to others (even though I forget to ask myself).
- I love being the number two or the kingmaker. Support is my sweet spot (and it feels good to be needed by someone important).
- I'm more comfortable giving than receiving, but I would like a little applause for my generosity.
- When it comes to taking care of others, I don't always know how—or when—to say no. I worry about what they'll think of me.
- When people ask what I need or how I feel, I have no idea how to answer. It takes me a while to find my own feelings under everyone else's.
- Getting things ready for others is a literal joy... until I realize no one noticed.

- When I'm tired, I feel like people take me for granted. Then I secretly fume about it—then worry whether they still like me.
- I hide my own needs to keep things peaceful and to make sure everyone still wants me around.
- "Honestly? I don't need anything." Except a thank-you would be nice.
- I'm always charming. But I can use flattery to get acceptance.
- I worry about miscommunication, but I soften my words so much that sometimes no one knows what I meant.
- I spend a lot of mental energy thinking about relationships. (Including this one. Right now.)
- I'm a great coach. I can rub your back and kick your ass at the same time. And you'll thank me for it.
- Beneath it all, I want to know I'm worthy of love—even when I'm not helping.

Three Shifts That Build Joy and Strength for Enneagram Twos

1. **Make "What is mine to do?" your first question.** You assume your help is needed or requested. Because you're subconsciously attuned to the wishes and wants of others, you often jump in to support or offer advice. This overfunctioning is a form of pride. I know...but think about it from a different viewpoint. There's an arrogance in believing you know what other people need better than they do.

   If you're practicing ruthless self-honesty, you're helping so you're sure they always want you around and they notice your help. But the truth is, you are loved even if you don't help everyone before they ask. Your worth isn't dependent upon other people's view of you. You are worthy to love yourself without other people's validation.

   These questions will guide you when you feel yourself jumping in to help:
   - What is mine to do?
   - Did this person ask for my help?
   - Did I agree to help or just assume?
   - Who owns this problem?
   - What needs my attention right now?

   (Make this your phone lockscreen if you need to!)

2. **Practicing caring for yourself—possibly before others.** When you deny or neglect your needs, you are hurting yourself and the thing you care about the most, your relationships. When you don't ask for what you need from others or you sacrifice your needs to help other people, you distance yourself from the people you want love from the most. (You might want to read that again and let it sink in. It's a little mind-blowing.)

   Rejecting your own needs results in overstepping with unwanted advice or intrusive behaviors that push people away. You can lean into emotional manipulation and play the martyr. Before you slide down the shame spiral, hear me: this is mostly unconscious. Which is why you've got to pay attention when these behaviors show up. They're a signal you are neglecting your own humanity.

   If you are caring for yourself, you are practicing the self-love that diminishes your need to clamor for the love and appreciation of others. You've got to build that muscle of loving yourself and directly asking for what you need. The first step is to get curious about yourself, so you become as intuitive about yourself as you are about others. Then you can ask others for what you actually need from them.

- Start your day with a morning ritual that is just for you. Ask yourself, What would I like from today?
- Set reminders on your phone to pop up a couple of times a day with these questions: What am I feeling right now? What do I need right now? Bonus points if you write down the answers.
- Directly ask for what you want from others. No dropping hints or giving options you don't actually want. Don't calculate what's the easiest for them, what will flatter them, or hedge with "oh, but you don't have to." "I need some help. Could you [direct ask]?" and wait. (You can do it.)

3. **Boundaries will change your life.** Because the lines between you and others can be blurry, boundaries are often an issue for you. In your desire to help, you sometimes take responsibility for things that belong to other people: emotions, problems, tasks, consequences, and more. And left unchecked, it will lead to unmet expectations, overfunctioning, and even codependency.

You are responsible *for* yourself. You are responsible *to* other people. When you have blurry boundaries, your Two personality wants you to be responsible for other people, so they'll like you. This happens at work, at home, at the grocery store. And without boundaries, your joy is dependent on the whims of others.

When requests are made, practice with some verbal boundaries:

- Use "maybe." Since you often jump in with yes and no feels rude, ease in with maybe.
- That doesn't work for me right now. You don't have to apologize, but I can imagine that sentence feels incomplete for you. You can add, "I wish I could help."
- No is a complete sentence. You don't have to explain every choice you make. Own your decision and let the other person be responsible for their reactions and choices.

One more thing: Joy grows when you love yourself the way you love everyone else.

Three: The Successful Inventor

Threes believe they have to look successful to other people because it's not ok to have their own identity. They use identification or image-crafting to avoid failure and to maintain a self-image of being successful. Threes want to be worthy without the work, but they'll settle for a chart of gold stars.

If You're an **Enneagram Three** You'll Get This

- I believe I'll be okay as long as I'm crushing a new goal.
- "I've got this." (And I usually do.)
- I make killer first impressions—I practically sparkle on arrival. (And I know exactly who has the most influence when I walk in.)
- I love my job. Actually, I am my job.
- I'm really good at looking like I'm having fun, but I don't remember the last time I had fun without a purpose.
- I'm not saying I'm competitive, but I've definitely turned therapy into a performance review.
- I can find a way to win over and connect with almost anyone. I have a persona for every room I walk into. I'm not inauthentic; I'm adaptable.
- I go hard... then crash like a sugar-high kid after the party's over.
- "Don't talk to me while I'm working" should be on a sign above my desk.
- I'm truly baffled when others don't chase their dreams with the same enthusiasm that I chase mine.
- I track my sales numbers, my steps, and my success metrics. When I hit the goal, then I'll celebrate. (Okay, when I hit the next goal. I mean, the next one.)
- I'm great at appearing confident, but sometimes I feel more like a brand than a person. Do other people think I am too?
- I'm all in on efficiency—even if it means a few creative shortcuts.
- My superpower? Turning ideas and dreams into measurable goals and progress charts.
- Beneath all the drive and charm, I really want to be loved for who I am, not just what I accomplish.

Three Shifts That Build Joy and Strength for Enneagram Threes

1. **See people as humans.** Other people aren't either your tools to success or your competition. This either/or comes from a scarcity mindset that tells you there's not enough to go around. So you compete to be the best or use people on the path to success. I know that's not who you are, but your personality pushes you there.

You'll notice this when you experience impatience or an internal rushing feeling, like when other people are telling a story or asking questions that seem inefficient. You'll want to work on your story around this (See SNAP in chapter 3.).

In the moment, try this:

Physically: Wiggle your toes in your shoes and take a slow and take a deep silent breath. This will bring you back into your body and out of the future in your mind.

Emotionally: Leave room for feelings. Your impatience is a mix of anxiety (What if this slows down the way to the goal?), irritation (I shouldn't have to listen to this.), and a touch of shame (I shouldn't feel this way.). Remember feelings are data, not a roadblock. Name them and let them go.

Mentally: Remind yourself—As much as I want to be valued, so does this person. You will have more joy and hope in connection.

2. **Become radical about the truth.** The vainglory fixation of your personality will have you padding your resume, inflating your connections, or leaving out some information that lets people assume what you want them to see about you. When you invent this persona, you're separating from your real self and even piling on shame that your real self isn't good enough to be seen.

When you feel the need to embellish (or diminish), ask yourself:
What is the fullest truth here?
What am I feeling right now?
How am I am spinning the events or connection so I look good?

Start small and build this muscle by sharing with other people. Choose trusted people to reveal yourself to—people who will listen without judgement and tell you the truth about yourself (aside from your achievements).

As you practice sharing your real feelings and ideas with your closest people, you'll continue to connect with your favorite self that isn't motivated to invent a more impressive image.

3. **Practice failure.** I get that even considering this might strike at your heart. Which is why you to need practice experiencing failures to see you're still loved and significant regardless—and even because of—the failure.

Failure is inevitable and always part of the process. And you've probably spent months or even years avoiding and hiding failure. I've found that Threes who continue to sidestep failure are ultimately filled with more shame and experience fewer successes. Your personality says you won't be worthy if people see your shortcomings, but the truth is the connection is in the imperfections.

For the next 6 weeks, do something that feels uncomfortable or embarrassing. Simple and small. Take a selfie with a horrible expression or no makeup and post it on social media for 24 hours. Sing karaoke. Dance down the aisle at Costco. Write what you tried and how it felt.

☐ How did you feel?	☐ How did you feel?
☐ How did you feel?	☐ How did you feel?
☐ How did you feel?	☐ How did you feel?

If you do at least 1 every week for 6 weeks, give yourself a reward (because you still love a gold star!).

Reward:

One more thing: Joy will grow when you stop performing and just start being.

Four: The Romantic Individualist

Fours believe they have to be authentic because it's not ok to be not enough or too much. They use introjection (taking in others' feelings as their own) and amplification (making everything bigger) to avoid ordinariness and to maintain a self-image of being authentic. Fours want to be known, but they'll settle for being noticed.

If You're an **Enneagram Four,** You'll Get This

- I've been called "emotionally intense."
- I have an aesthetic.
- Nostalgia is my favorite season.
- All I want is to live a deep, purposeful, emotionally rich life—one where I express myself through beauty and authenticity. Is that really too much to ask?
- I'm always ready for the deep, real conversation. I can hold space for anyone. But chit chat? Nightmare.
- I compare myself to others constantly. I'm always too much and not enough, the black sheep and the masterpiece.
- Melancholy feels safe to me. Why do people want to cheer me up?
- I'm sensitive to criticism—especially about my work. It feels personal because my work is an expression of my core self.
- I have so many feelings in a day it's hard to know which one to experience first.
- I expect people to share in the romantic moment they don't realize is happening.
- When people tell me what to do, my first instinct is "absolutely not."
- I'm wildly imaginative. I come up with one brilliant idea after another. Now, getting them done is a different story...
- "Come here. Go away. Don't leave." You're the yo-yo, and I'm the hand rejecting or reeling you in, unsure whether you'll love me or leave me.
- I'm not like everyone else. (And I'm both proud and lonely about that.)
- I want to be seen and loved for who I really am.

Three Shifts That Build Joy and Strength for Enneagram Fours

1. **Decide your emotions are not facts.** Don't throw the book! Your feelings are true, valid, and a real experience. And if you remember chapter 6 in *Joyosity*, your emotions are your stories about an experience.

   Allow your emotions to be valid but not the only data point you use to live.

Engage your Thinking Center of Intelligence to examine the story (see SNAP in chapter 3). Ask yourself some questions:

- *What am I assuming about myself or other people?*
- *How can I view this more objectively?*
- *This feeling is temporary. What do I want when this feeling has passed?*

Find emotional outlets. As a Four, your emotions tend to hang around for the afterparty. You need to find a way to show them out the door. Creative outlets, journaling, especially something physical, will help you process your emotions instead of spiraling in them.

Write a few ways you like to process emotions here.

2. **Believe you have everything you need inside of you.** Your envy stands on top of shame that will flat-out lie to you. It whispers, "See how you're struggling. You don't have what it takes. Everyone else knows how to do this." The truth is that everyone messes up all the time, no one has it all figured out, and you aren't different or hopelessly flawed because you struggle.

You'll notice this steals your joy because you're imagining living someone else's life rather that creating your own beauty in the world. Here are red flag thoughts that mean you're stuck in the envy trap.

If I could do _____ like _____, then I could be happy.

If only had_____, then I could be truly happy.

I will be happy when___.

Notice the pattern? You're looking for something outside of you to bring joy and happiness to you.

Search your memory for a time when you didn't compare yourself or your circumstances to others. Describe it here. What were you doing? How did you feel? Include as much rich detail as possible, especially the emotional layers, your thoughts, and your actions.

When you notice your red flag thoughts, come back to this experience. Remind your heart and mind you have everything you need inside of you because you've done it before.

3. **Keep an Achievement Archive.** You've been licking that old wound of rejection and inferiority for a long time, so melancholy and seeing what's missing feels cozy

and safe. You need a new mental focus to see the joy that's readily available to you Develop a habit of archiving the wins, successes, and moments when you are proud of yourself. This will feel all kinds of awkward at first because your mental model has carved a deep rut into what's lacking, so you've ignored positives. Both coexist, but you need to build new mental habits to see the good.

Get a notebook and pen that live next to your bed. Before you turn off the light at night, record 1 thing you did that day you're proud of. It can be super simple like, "I hung my shirt up instead of leaving it on 'the chair.'" It can also be bigger, "I communicated details clearly in the meeting today." It can also be deeper: "I am a good friend."

This habit builds your capacity to see the positives in your life and the beauty you create in the world.

One more thing: You are already enough to experience joy.

Head Group: Fives, Sixes, Sevens

Primary Emotional Struggle: Fear and Isolation
Deepest Desires: Security and Safety

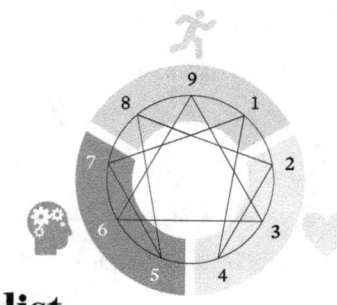

Five: The Curious Specialist

Fives believe they have to be competent because it's not ok to let their guard down and be too comfortable. They use isolation and intellectualization to avoid depletion and to maintain a self-image of being knowledgeable. Fives want to be safe in the unknown, but they'll settle for being the competent expert.

If You're an **Enneagram Five,** You'll Get This

+ Knowledge is power and protection. I'm endlessly curious—and endlessly tired.
+ I want to understand life at every level: mental, emotional, physical. (Mostly mental.)
+ I have high standards for research and a low tolerance for nonsense.
+ Thoughts are reliable. Feelings—yours or mine—less so.
+ Sometimes I forget I have an actual body; I'm in my mind castle.
+ I want to be the wise one—competent, autonomous, never needy. I'm self-sufficient to a fault. I can take care of myself; you should too.
+ People say I seem calm. I'm actually just conserving energy.
+ I'm all about strategy and decision-trees. "I'll think about that and get back to you." = "I'm going to research it for hours."

+ If I have to be in a group, I'd rather observe. Small talk is my kryptonite.
+ I'm awkward in groups, but if you ask about my niche obsession, good luck getting me to stop.
+ I have inside jokes with myself. I don't know why people are surprised that I'm funny, because honestly, I'm hilarious.
+ I isolate to protect myself because people's needs feel like black holes of energy.
+ I fall into the trap of scarcity, where the fear of depletion is what depletes me.
+ I want to master a subject, but I'll never think I know enough to call myself an expert.
+ Beneath it all, I'm just trying to feel safe enough to feel comfortable.

Three Shifts That Build Joy and Strength for Enneagram Fives

1. **Act before you feel ready.** Your personality says you don't have enough information or a detailed enough plan. The truth is you've likely already gathered more information than you need and no plan is foolproof.

   When you go down the research (or Reddit) rabbit hole, it's less about finding more information than about indulging your need for knowledge. Also, remember having a plan is not the same as acting on the plan.

   Give yourself a deadline. When you have a decision or project, create a deadline for when it's time to act. This can be a date on the calendar or a time limit. I will decide by this date, or I will spend this amount of time gathering information and planning. When the deadline comes, start acting. (You can always adjust as you go.)

2. **Identify and experience your feelings.** It's not that you don't have emotions, it's just that you trust your logic and thoughts so much more. So it feels infinitely more comfortable to think about your feelings and intellectualize them rather than experience them.

   When you disconnect from your emotions, you separate from your body, other people, and joy. And they hang around anyway, showing up in your body. They come out sideways in relationships, or you feel numb to everything.

   Pick 3 days in a row to reconnect with emotions. Set a reminder in your phone or calendar at the top of every hour. Ask:

   - *What am I feeling right now?*
   - *What else am I feeling?*
   - *Am I feeling anything else?*
   - *Where am I feeling it in my body?*

   Use Name-Rate-Find in chapter 5 so you're not intellectualizing feelings but practicing experiencing emotions and letting them move through.

3. **Stretch your ability to engage.** By habit, you tend to withdraw in most settings. You prefer to observe from outside the group—because goodness! it takes all that energy to be in the group. That's scarcity and avarice talking. You have more energy to give than you think; you simply have to practice it.

   Your personality tells you that if you engage with people, they'll need more of you than you can give. First, you must change your story around this, or you won't even want to engage (see SNAP in chapter 3). Next, you have to prove to your body and mind that you can do it. Start small and extremely granular.

For the next two weeks, when you attend any gathering of people (socially or professionally), do this:

- Choose a spot to sit or stand in the middle of where folks are congregating, not the fringes.
- Make casual eye contact and smile. This means they will likely smile back or even approach you.
- When someone comes toward you, greet them (introduce yourself if you don't know them) and engage by asking a question. Try: What's been the best part of your day so far? Have you read anything interesting recently? What are you looking forward to right now?
- You can also share your answers.
- Be proud of yourself and take some alone time.

If that feels easy to you, practice sharing your ideas with other people and asking for feedback. This will increase your interdependence and connection with others (and also improve your ideas).

One more thing: You can't research your way to joy. It's safe to step out and let it surprise you.

Six: The Loyal Skeptic

Sixes believe they have to be loyal and prepared because it's not ok to trust themselves. They use projection (putting their own doubts onto others) and anticipation to avoid personal rejection and to maintain a self-image of being loyal. Sixes want to have security, but they'll settle for being the ever-ready supporter.

If You're an **Enneagram Six,** You'll Get This

+ I'm clutch in a crisis, but when it's over, I completely fall apart.
+ I've absolutely planned out 16 different potential scenarios and contingency plans. Sometimes I forget *The Worst-Case Scenario Survival Handbook* is satire, not a guidebook.
+ It makes me nervous when people aren't prepared. (Please, just pack the umbrella.)
+ People say I'm loyal, witty, and dependable—which is true. Also: anxious, cautious, and caffeinated.
+ I'm a world-class troubleshooter. I play devil's advocate, but only because I want things to succeed.
+ "I have another question." (Of course I do.)
+ I crave certainty. I second-guess authority, systems, and anyone who seems too confident. And, sometimes, I protect myself by deciding you're all good or all bad.
+ "Do you think I should...?" is basically my catchphrase. I'm great at giving advice, and terrible at taking my own.
+ I don't really want to run the show. But I do want to hire the director.
+ I can read people quickly, and usually people can read me. My emotions are on my face.
+ I'm skeptical of flattery. Why are you being so nice to me? What do you want?
+ I'm loyal as all get out—ride or die, even when it's inconvenient. And I stand by people longer than is probably wise.
+ I want to trust myself as much as other people trust me.
+ I do know that I'm brave. It's hard to remember that when I'm shaking while I do it.
+ Beneath all the worry, I just want to feel safe.

Three Shifts That Build Joy and Strength for Enneagram Sixes

1. **Practice intentional worry.** You're already scenario-building. But it's underneath your consciousness, running in the background but still crowding your heart and mind. So instead of letting the hamster stay stuck on the wheel, you need to bring the worry up into your attention.

   - First, get a Worries and Wins journal, a small notebook you can carry with you. (Resist doing this on your phone or computer, but that will work in a pinch!)

   - When you notice you're scenario-building, grab the journal and set a timer for 15 minutes. Date the page and start focusing on your worries. Write as much as you can about your worries for the full amount of time. Number them. Flesh them out. Record all the details of your worries and anxieties about what might happen. Typically, you'll feel the urge to choose an action step before the 15 minutes are up but keep going for the full 15. If the timer goes off while you're writing, pencil down. Close the journal. Take a deep inhale and exhale. Go on to your next task.

   - Once a month, flip back through your worries. Make note of any of the scenarios that came true and how you responded. You'll notice a couple of things. Very few scenarios happened, and you handled those well.

   Use this to build the muscle that you can trust yourself to make good choices.

2. **Watch out for us and them.** Because you are fiercely loyal to your group, two problems easily come up: You see your group as your identity, and an "if you're not with us, you're against us" posture.

   If you aren't aware, you will be devastated by changes in group dynamics and the natural ebb and flow of friendships or work relationships. And if you see people as against you because they don't belong to your group (or as a way to protect your belonging and safety in a group), you'll start to see other people as threatening, their contributions as invalid, and even their humanity not as worthy as yours. Now, I know this isn't what you want do. Particularly if you are a leader, "othering" people will hurt your team and your career. So that's why you've got to be cautious of this tendency of your personality. While it's trying to keep you safe, it's cutting you off from the joy of diverse relationships.

- Develop your identity, needs, wants, interests, opinions, and values as an individual, not only part of your group or community. Your safety isn't at stake because you aren't 100% like the group. Start by completing the NAVIGATE exercise from chapter 4—without getting input from other people.
- Focus on the human in front of you. Spend less time wondering if they are trustworthy or not and relax into kindness. Take a grounding breath and ask a curious question without doing an internal risk analysis or creating a "what if they say this" plan.

3. **Develop a healthier relationship with authority.** Sixes often fall into a reactive response to authority figures—bosses, mentors, coaches, teachers, etc. The reactions tend toward the extremes of blind trust or mechanical rebellion.

   Just because your boss seems to have a negative response to something you do, that doesn't mean your job or relationship is in jeopardy. And on the flipside, if a team lead asks you to adjust your work, firing off a message like, "Well, maybe next time I'll do nothing," is unhelpful.

   - Develop self-trust (see number 1 above.) You don't need to latch onto an authority to compensate for your self-doubt.
   - Remove the parent-child frame of authority. While the authority may have more responsibility or influence, you are not a child. You are adults in a working relationship, each with skills, gifts, and agency to contribute.
   - Be on the alert for these childish behaviors and practice replacing them with the leadership behaviors.

Childish Behavior	Leadership Behavior
Over-apologize	Own what is yours and don't assume blame for everything. Use confident, short statements: "Thanks for catching that. I'll fix it."
Gossip or complain to peers	Go directly to share the impact of a statement or action and ask for clarity or an adjustment. Don't share others' information to gain loyalty.
Ask for guidance or approval for everything	Make decisions within your assigned authority. Ask for guidance after thinking it through.
Assume they always know best	Respond with curiosity and confidence. "Are you open to another way? I have an idea."

Being the pleaser. (Jump. How high?)	Collaborate as an equal. Consider both your needs and expertise as well as theirs.
Take any feedback as fault or disapproval.	Receive feedback as investment in you, helping you grow in self-trust.
Use baby talk or childish tone.	Communicate as an equal with steady confidence.
Hide mistakes so you don't disappoint.	Acknowledge your mistake and fix it. Everyone makes mistakes; how you fix them is the differentiator.
Over-question and reflexively challenge.	Start with "OK" instead of "No, that won't work." Then rank your questions based on what you need to know most to move forward.
Pout, shut down, or withdraw until they come to you.	Acknowledge the difficulty but stay engaged. Address what you need, and don't wait to be rescued or pursued.
Which on this list are you prone to?	

One more thing: As you trust yourself, joy turns the unknown into possibility.

Seven: The Enthusiastic Visionary

Sevens believe they have to be ok and joyful because it's not ok to depend on others to take care of them. They use rationalization and reframing to avoid suffering and to maintain a self-image of being OK. Sevens want enduring contentment, but they'll settle for thrills.

If You're an **Enneagram Seven,** You'll Get This

+ I'm the eternal optimist. I'd roast s'mores in Hades.

+ I've booked the plane tickets, the hotel, and an excursion to avoid doing my taxes.

+ Enthusiastic is my middle name. (My other middle name is distracted.) I'm already planning the next great meal while I'm still at the supper table.

+ Brainstorming is my superpower. I can create options. Always.

+ I believe I can convince you to see it my way. I'm not bending the rules— I'm improving them.

+ I'm allergic to boredom, limits, and other people's heavy vibes. If I just keep moving from one exciting thing to the next, the hard stuff can't catch me.

+ Honestly, people worry too much. You can reframe almost anything into a positive. (It's a gift and a coping mechanism.)

+ I'm not afraid of failure, but I am terrified of disappointment.

+ Nothing triggers me faster than the illogical negative emotions of other people. Just fix it!

+ When the difficult emotions I've run from finally show up, my tears come in the car, on the pillow, or during a really good commercial.

+ Sometimes, I get tired of being the life of the party on demand. I'm frustrated when people think I'm shallow and don't see the depth under the fun.

+ I love everyone, but I don't really need anyone.

+ I don't like commitments on the spot— what if something better comes up?

+ My idealism is genuine: comfort and change-agent but also escape hatch and shadow-dodger.

+ Beneath all the fun, I just want to feel free and at peace.

Three Shifts That Build Joy and Strength for Enneagram Sevens

1. **Give your responsibilities rhythms.** Adulting feels so boring and limiting, but you can't outrun it. Eventually you will have no joy because you're trapped by the pile-up effect of avoidance.

Create a regular time to take care of your toil (or even what's in the messy middle). Make it fun and something you look forward to by pairing it with something you enjoy. Save your coffee points for your weekly finance review on Fridays. Go to your favorite location to complete your expense reports on Wednesdays. Listen to your current favorite album while reviewing your calendar for the week. (See Rhythms in chapter 10.)

Track the impact over time of taking care of your toil:

WEEK ONE:									
How do I feel about this task?									
1	2	3	4	5	6	7	8	9	10
THE WORST									I LOVE IT
Words to describe how I feel:									
How is my overall life right now?									
1	2	3	4	5	6	7	8	9	10
AWFUL									THE BEST
Words to describe how I feel:									

WEEK TWO:									
How do I feel about this task?									
1	2	3	4	5	6	7	8	9	10
THE WORST									I LOVE IT
Words to describe how I feel:									
How is my overall life right now?									
1	2	3	4	5	6	7	8	9	10
AWFUL									THE BEST
Words to describe how I feel:									

WEEK THREE:									
How do I feel about this task?									
1	2	3	4	5	6	7	8	9	10
THE WORST									I LOVE IT
Words to describe how I feel:									
How is my overall life right now?									
1	2	3	4	5	6	7	8	9	10
AWFUL									THE BEST
Words to describe how I feel:									

WEEK FOUR:									
How do I feel about this task?									
1	2	3	4	5	6	7	8	9	10
THE WORST									I LOVE IT
Words to describe how I feel:									
How is my overall life right now?									
1	2	3	4	5	6	7	8	9	10
AWFUL									THE BEST
Words to describe how I feel:									

WEEK FIVE:									
How do I feel about this task?									
1	2	3	4	5	6	7	8	9	10
THE WORST									I LOVE IT
Words to describe how I feel:									
How is my overall life right now?									
1	2	3	4	5	6	7	8	9	10
AWFUL									THE BEST
Words to describe how I feel:									

WEEK SIX:									
How do I feel about this task?									
1	2	3	4	5	6	7	8	9	10
THE WORST									I LOVE IT
Words to describe how I feel:									
How is my overall life right now?									
1	2	3	4	5	6	7	8	9	10
AWFUL									THE BEST
Words to describe how I feel:									

WEEK SEVEN:									
How do I feel about this task?									
1	2	3	4	5	6	7	8	9	10
THE WORST									I LOVE IT
Words to describe how I feel:									
How is my overall life right now?									
1	2	3	4	5	6	7	8	9	10
AWFUL									THE BEST
Words to describe how I feel:									

2. **Learn to experience the feelings of discomfort and disappointment.** The feeling of difficult or uncomfortable emotions will not last forever. I know, it feels like forever, but remember from chapter 6 in *Joyosity*, they pass through in 6-90 seconds if you allow them to process.

For Sevens, it's helpful to get data about how long emotions really last.

When you practice Name-Rate-Find, start a stopwatch. When you have named the emotions and feelings all the way through finding them in your body and the physical intensity lowers, stop the stopwatch.

How long was the process? Did you make it through?

You'll find it's rarely longer than 90 seconds. And when you notice you're avoiding sitting with emotions, remind yourself it won't last forever. And now you have data to back it up.

*Note: Do not rush through this. It's not, beat your best time situation! Sometimes it takes longer, but it's never forever.

3. **Listen fully, all the way to the end.** As a Seven, your excitability and self-referencing can get in the way of real connection and communication. People sometimes come away feeling like they've been to a story-time performance, or even worse, dismissed by your interruptions or topping their story. You want the conversation to be a joint adventure, not one-sided.

   Instead of interrupting, practice what David Brooks calls being a "loud listener." Actively listen with "oohs and aahs and wows and nos." Let your excitability stay focused on the other person. When they stop, take an extra breath, then reflect back what you heard and ask a follow-up question.

   The Extra Mile: Get feedback from someone else who will tell you the truth. After a conversation, ask these questions. Note, this isn't for you to agree or disagree. Simply see what other people notice.

   What do you think our talking time ratio was? How much did I talk, and how much did you talk?

   Did you notice any time I interrupted, redirected, seemed distracted, or wasn't listening?

One more thing: When you stop running from pain, joy deepens instead of disappearing.

Keep trying out the Enneagram in your life, but always focus on the motivations, not the behavior. And sometimes you want more support with an expert with you in real-time. Go to jennwhitmer.com/enneagram to find out about an Enneagram Navigator session or coaching.

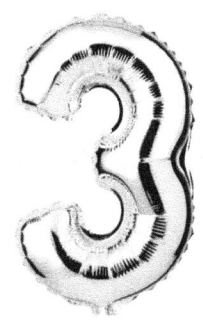

Write New Plays and Change the Game

In *Joyosity*, you learned you are wired for narrative. Because your brain is hardwired to create that story, the meaning you chose is the story you live in. And those stories determine results. The meaning you create is how you decide what actions you need to take. And your actions determine your outcomes.

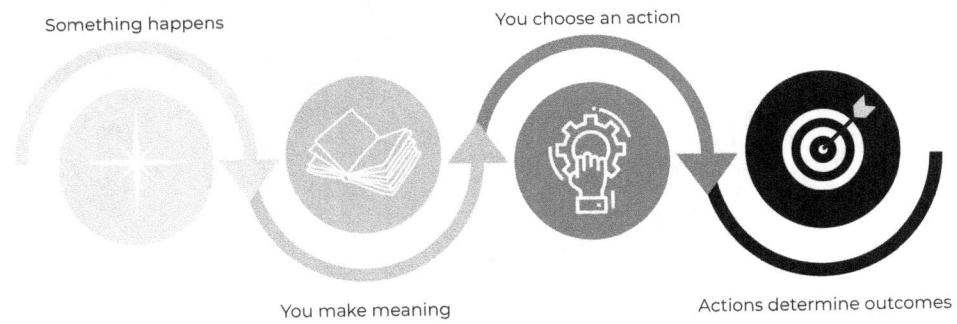

You can reliably change the story in your mind. Not every thought you have is true. But if you keep telling yourself that story, you'll believe it's true. Use SNAP to change the story. Stop, Notice, Ask, Pivot.

Stop	Pause and breathe.
Notice	Who, what, when, and where. Observe how you feel.
Ask	What story am I believing right now? Is it true? What could happen if I believed a different story?
Pivot	Choose a new action.

We're going to dig into the nitty gritty of the Story Transformation Process: Using self-efficacy and the Enneagram to rewrite with truth.

Self-Efficacy

Self-efficacy is your ability to believe you have the capacity or capability you need. It's specific and targeted at helping you believe you have the agency to achieve what you want. Self-efficacy gives you reality-based options for rewriting stories. In other words, self-efficacy is the skill of confidence.

Ideally you have options for all 5 components of self-efficacy: your own previous experience, vicarious experience from others, visualization and imagined experience, coaching and feedback, and self-regulation. When you are rewriting, use 1 or a mixture of these 5 components to reduce the discrepancy and increase your brain's acceptance of the new story.

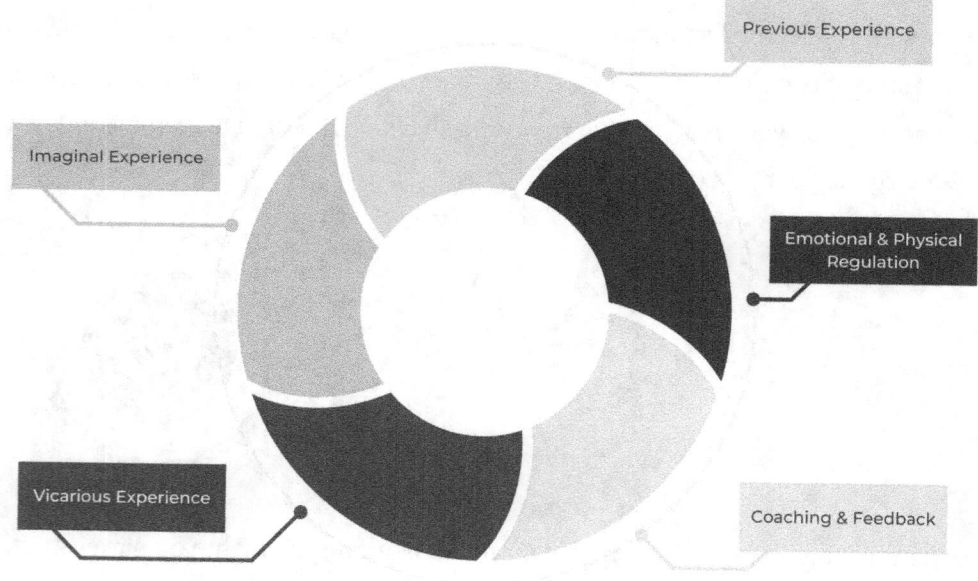

Previous Experience

I've done it before, I can do it again

What you've done before and experienced in your life is the most reliable evidence for your brain. When you are looking for previous experiences, go back to times when you've been successful in a similar situation.

Let's say your story is "I always give terrible presentations." Find a time when you gave a small presentation well. You now have evidence to build a new story. "I can give good presentations." Or even further, "I give good presentations." When you pull from your previous experiences, it's like editing a first draft and not rewriting an entirely new story.

Vicarious Experience

If you can do it, I can too.

When you see someone like you succeeding, your body recognizes this as possible for you. When you are rewriting your story, and you can't find evidence in your experience, find someone else who's done it. It could be a friend or mentor you know in real life, but it can also be Guiding Voices that we'll talk about in chapter 8 on decisions. Borrow their experience and put it into your story.

Imaginal Experience

I can picture doing this.

Visualization has long been used in sports to improve physical skills. In a test with tennis players, researchers found that imagining the performance significantly improved the actual performance of the tennis player's ability to return serves. And it continues with hockey players, Olympians, and even my high school swim team on the pool deck, practicing flip turns in our minds. Imagining the positive experience improves performance.

When you rewrite with truth, you can pull from your imagination before you've had the new experience. Imagine the outcomes, the emotions, how you'll stand. You can even rehearse in a mirror, so your body has the physical practice. Imagine asking for the salary you want. And then say it out loud, over and over, rewriting the story by imagining it.

Remember, it has to be based in reality. You can't just imagine someone giving you buckets of cash. But you can imagine asking for a 10% raise and a title bump.

Coaching and Feedback

What do you see?

You can't see your own magic. Like the habits that wreak havoc because they are in your Blind Spot, your magic lives there too. And if you remember the Johari window Blind Spot, you need feedback to get to Open.

Sometimes it's hard to see a new story. You need the help of coaching to see new possibilities and feedback to more accurately see yourself. (More in chapter 8 on choosing your Personal Board of feedback givers.)

Ask people you trust—and are kind—to tell you the truth:

- *Right now, the story I'm telling myself is this.*
- *What are other ways I can see this?*
- *What else do you see?*
- *How would you see this?*

Emotional and Physical Regulation

I'm running this show.

A key part of self-efficacy—emotional and physical regulation—is knowing when you're capable of rewriting the story. Is now the right time?

Part of emotional and physical regulation is knowing when it's time to stop—like the first part of SNAP is to *stop and breathe*. That's being in charge of your own body and being able to label your emotions. It's part of the Notice step—managing your emotional regulation in real time.

Let me be clear: in the middle of a meeting, when you feel activated and elevated and like you're about ready to throw your phone across the room? That is *not* the time to dig into rewriting a story.

You may need to wait some—until you can manage your emotions and get your body under control. (This key people power skill in *Joyosity* has more tools in chapter 5.)

You get to be the one in charge of all the aspects of your being. You've been in the meeting where the boss flies off the handle. You definitely don't walk away thinking, "Now that is someone in control and confident."

That's why this is such a crucial part of leadership and self-efficacy: it's not only about managing the *stories* in your mind. It's also about managing your *body* and your *emotions*.

Swapping the Enneagram Stories

Often, your Enneagram Silent Script is one of the stories you're believing. But telling yourself to believe your Enneagram Sustaining Story isn't enough. You need to connect the new story with one of the areas of self-efficacy. As a quick review, here are the Silent Scripts and Sustaining Stories by type.

Eight	Nine	One
Silent Script: It's not OK to trust anyone.	*Silent Script*: It's not OK to assert myself.	*Silent Script*: It's not OK to make mistakes.
Sustaining Story: I am wise enough to trust the right people who won't betray me. I do not have to fight for my belonging. It's OK to be vulnerable.	*Sustaining Story*: My presence matters. People want to hear what I have to say. I still belong when I engage with others, even when I assert myself.	*Sustaining Story*: I am good, even in imperfection. If someone else catches my mistake, I still have respect and belonging in the group

Two	Three	Four
Silent Script: It's not OK for me to have my own needs.	*Silent Script*: It's not OK to have my own feelings or identity.	*Silent Script*: It's not OK to be too functional or too happy.
Sustaining Story: I am wanted. My emotional and physical needs are part of my humanity, and I can put them first. People will still love me when I express my needs.	*Sustaining Story*: I am loved for just being me. My accomplishments don't determine my value. I can share my feelings and still have worth.	*Sustaining Story*: I am seen for who I am. I am not too much. I am enough. It's OK for me to find joy in the world and take care of myself.

Five	Six	Seven
Silent Script: It's not OK to be comfortable in the world.	*Silent Script*: It's not OK to trust yourself.	*Silent Script*: It's not OK to depend on anyone for anything.
Sustaining Story: My needs are not a problem to solve. It's OK for me to be comfortable with people and take care of my body. I am safe to ask for help from other people and when I act before I've gathered all the information.	*Sustaining Story*: I can trust my judgments. I am safe. I can rest and let life unfold, knowing I can handle whatever comes my way.	*Sustaining Story*: I will be taken care of. I can experience discomfort or pain without distractions. I can experience difficulty and still be safe.

Shift the Script ⏱ 10-20 *minutes*

Stories are sticky in your brain, especially when there are sensory and emotional details. When you are building a new story, you need one that's just as clingy as your Silent Script. As you work through this exercise, don't overthink it. Write what pops into your mind. You can come back to expand or deepen.

Here's an example, followed by a blank framework and instructions for your own story work.

Sustaining Story:	
I am good, even in imperfection. If someone else catches my mistake, I still have respect and belonging in the group.	
Times when this story was true.	**What happened? How did I feel?**
During a team report, Jill noticed a typo in a client's name on my slide. I thanked her for pointing it out. I fixed it, and we moved on to the next thing.	No one said anything rude. Shondra empathized and named that it feels awkward, but mistakes happen and that's why we have a team to help us. I felt relief and connection.

Imagine for a moment this story always true. How would you show up differently? What actions will you take?

I'd relax more in collaboration, take feedback with curiosity, and celebrate progress instead of delaying until everything is perfect. I could spend less time after hours working.

When I feel the urge to keep tweaking, I will ask for feedback: "Is this good enough to move on?"

Your Turn to Shift the Script

- Write your Enneagram Sustaining Story in the top box.
- Find previous experiences or vicarious experiences when this story was true. Name at least 2 situations.
- Record the outcomes and how you felt (or would feel).
- Create an imaginal experience and identify a new action that comes from that story.

If you're struggling, get some coaching or feedback from one of those trusted kind people.

Sustaining Story:

Times when this story was true.	What happened? How did I feel?

Imagine for a moment this story always true. How would you show up differently? What actions will you take?

The Extra Mile: Write your sustaining story and action on a note card. Read the card every morning for 30 days (or as long as you want!)

I am (or I can) [sustaining story] so I will [new action.]

_____

_____

_____

_____

Every time you stop, notice, ask, and pivot, you strengthen your ability to write a truer story that cultivates joy. This isn't a one-time edit; it's a daily practice of awareness and agency.

The more you practice SNAP and Shifting the Script, the more natural it becomes to live in the story that creates the most joy.

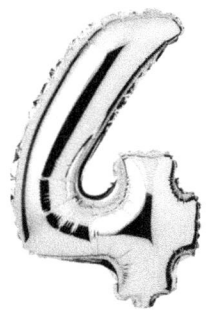

Define the Win and Play for It

In *Joyosity*, chapter 5 revealed how values are the lens through which you choose to see the world. They are the roots of your joy and the deep source of direction when everything else feels fuzzy. You saw how alignment between what you believe, say, and do builds integrity, connection, and purpose. Now, it's time to make that real.

This chapter moves you from knowing your values to naming, defining, and living them—so your choices, leadership, and joy all grow from the same strong roots. In this NAVIGATE process, you'll identify what truly matters to you, uncover the influences that shaped those beliefs, and translate your values into daily actions that create purpose, on purpose. It's time to navigate toward joy.

NOTE: If you've gone through a values exercise, I doubt this will be the process you've done before. In various iterations with audiences and workshops and executive coaching clients, every time, they say I've never done it like this before.

NAVIGATE Process steps:

Narrative Discovery

Authentic Alignment

Voice Your Values

Identify Meaning

Guide by Rank

Activate and Integrate

Transform and Evolve

Embody and Decide*

Entire process (you can break it up): ⏱ *2-3 hours*

Getting prepped

Time: When I do this at retreats, we take about 2 hours. You can also let this evolve over time. Block a couple of lunch times in a row to work or a few Saturday mornings. The longest sections will take you 30-45 minutes in 1 session.

Materials: You're going to need sticky notes or note cards. (I have a deep affinity for Post-its and a big wall, but you do what fits you). You can write in this book, use a white board, or grab your own journal or notebook. But this is not a keyboard exercise. The pen to paper (or even stylus to tablet) is an important part of the process.

Unity: Wherever you go, there you are. Which means, you only have one set of values. You don't have one for work and one for home. You may express those values differently at work than you do at home, but you do not hold different values. You want to live by those values in the conference room and in the dining room, especially when other people in the room hold different values.

Process: The process matters! **Don't skip steps.** Remember your values can evolve. You may want to refine and redefine. If you're stuck on an answer, get up. Go on a walk. Talk to somebody about it. Call a friend. Leave yourself a voice note. Don't sit and stare at a blank page.

No shame: We're uncovering your values here—not shaming you into them. I'm going to say this with very strong words right up front: *Release the guilt of not choosing family.* If your family doesn't show up as one of your top values, it doesn't mean you don't value your family.

---

*Adapted from Ken Black, Craig Pavlina, and Harris III.

This process requires you to be honest about *your own* values—you can't do that if you're ashamed of what your values actually are.

Dig a little: It's incredibly tempting to take the easy way out of this exercise and go with faith, hard work, family, or another "should" that comes from the influences of your culture, your workplace, or your family of origin. Be free to explore. Be curious about what's guiding you—and what lens you *want* to see the world through.

Narrative Discovery

Part One: Story ⏱ 15-20 *minutes*

What's your favorite movie? Or story, book, or, of course, musical? The one that when it happens to appear as you're flipping channels, you'll stop and watch. Or the novel you reread. The story that always brings out the feelings.

Favorite movie:

_____

What do you love about that movie? What are the reasons you like it?

_____
_____
_____

Who's the hero?   Who's the villain?   Who's the guide/best friend?

_____

What what's the main conflict, struggle, or problem?

_____
_____
_____

What what's the main plot in 1 to 3 sentences?

_____
_____
_____

When I first did this activity, I rejected it completely. Partly because I'm an Enneagram Seven who doesn't like to pick favorites. *Don't limit me!* Over time, I kept trying to do this exercise with a Top 10 list. It wasn't until I sat in a middle school theater, wiping tears from my eyes, I realized my favorite movie: *Newsies* (absolutely the 1992 version with Christian Bale).

I cried in my seat because the story points back to my values and purpose.

Newsies is an underdog story. Newsies were scraping by when the paper's owner gave in to greed and decided making more money was more important than the people. So the newsies banded together and said: *You have to treat us like people.* They figured out which strengths each newsie had, collaborated with others across the city, and came together for a giant rally for *all* the underrepresented and abused workers in 1890s New York City—and won.

With this frame, **go back and re-examine your favorite movie.**

You don't have to *change* your favorite movie. Find new elements in it: a struggle you wish didn't exist in the world, a quality you admire in the hero, something about the villain you want to eradicate from the world.

And if you want to take a little break, find your favorite clips from those movies.

The Extra Mile: Go talk about it with someone else—someone who either loves the movie or loves you. It's a great conversation starter, and it helps you connect the ideas more deeply to your life. Especially if it's someone who knows you well, they might offer insight about what they see in *you* that you didn't even notice as you reflect on the story.

Break time!

Part Two: Discovery Prompts ⏱ *20 minutes*

No one's coming to grade your work, so they don't have to be in complete sentences. Get your thoughts out of your head and onto the page.

I've found it incredibly effective to talk it out and move your body. It's powerful to move your body and contemplate at the same time because the part of your brain connected to thinking is also connected to your feet. Record a voice note while you walk or find the way that helps your ideas surface best. Make sure you capture your thoughts on paper at some point.

What accomplishments are you the proudest of?
What are your most meaningful experiences?
What are 2 or 3 things that are most important in your life?
What parts of your work and life do you never want to change?
What excites you or ignites passion in you?
What pisses you off more than anything else?
What are you willing to fight for?
What do you do or talk about that creates excitement in other people?
What do you do or talk about that creates advocates and enemies?
What kind of opportunities would you turn down based on principle?
What kind of things are you always willing to do? (Don't tell your boss, but you'd do it for free.)
What types of things will you never do? Even if they paid you!

If you're struggling with some of these, ask your kids, a sibling, or that uber-direct friend. They'll tell you!

Break time!

Authentic Alignment ⏱ *30-45 minutes*

Here comes the values list and Post-it party! Here are a few tips:

- *Go with your gut. Don't overthink it.*
- *There are no right or wrong answers. Don't shame yourself.*
- *Don't think about other people. Other people's ideas don't matter here—just yours.*

Step One: Cross & Circle

Use the Values List below. Cross out all the values you easily know "that's not it." Circle all the values that are who you want to be, how you want others to experience you, and how you want to see the world. (Don't worry about keeping this list tidy. It's in the Fillable Frameworks.)

Values List

Abundance	Acceptance	Accessibility	Accomplishment
Accountability	Accuracy	Achievement	Acknowledgement
Activeness	Adaptability	Adoration	Adroitness
Advancement	Adventure	Affection	Affluence
Aggressiveness	Agility	Alertness	Altruism
Amazement	Ambition	Amusement	Anticipation
Appreciation	Approachability	Approval	Art
Articulacy	Artistry	Assertiveness	Assurance
Attentiveness	Attractiveness	Audacity	Availability
Awareness	Awe	Balance	Beauty
Being the best	Belonging	Benevolence	Bliss
Boldness	Bravery	Brilliance	Buoyancy
Calmness	Camaraderie	Candor	Capability
Care	Carefulness	Celebrity	Certainty
Challenge	Change	Charity	Charm
Chastity	Cheerfulness	Clarity	Cleanliness
Clear mindedness	Cleverness	Closeness	Comfort
Commitment	Community	Compassion	Competence
Competition	Completion	Composure	Concentration
Confidence	Conformity	Congruency	Connection
Consciousness	Conservation	Consistency	Contentment
Continuity	Contribution	Control	Conviction
Conviviality	Coolness	Cooperation	Cordiality
Correctness	Country	Courage	Courtesy
Craftiness	Creativity	Credibility	Cunning
Curiosity	Daring	Decisiveness	Decorum
Deference	Delight	Dependability	Depth
Desire	Determination	Devotion	Devoutness
Dexterity	Dignity	Diligence	Direction
Directness	Discipline	Discovery	Discretion
Diversity	Dominance	Dreaming	Drive
Duty	Dynamism	Eagerness	Ease
Economy	Ecstasy	Education	Effectiveness
Efficiency	Elation	Elegance	Empathy
Encouragement	Endurance	Energy	Enjoyment
Entertainment	Enthusiasm	Environmentalism	Ethics
Euphoria	Excellence	Excitement	Exhilaration
Expectancy	Expediency	Experience	Expertise
Exploration	Expressiveness	Extravagance	Extroversion

Exuberance	Fairness	Faith	Fame
Family	Fascination	Fashion	Fearlessness
Ferocity	Fidelity	Fierceness	Financial Independence
Firmness	Fitness	Flexibility	Flow
Fluency	Focus	Fortitude	Frankness
Freedom	Friendliness	Friendship	Frugality
Fun	Gallantry	Generosity	Gentility
Giving	Grace	Gratitude	Gregariousness
Growth	Guidance	Happiness	Harmony
Health	Heart	Helpfulness	Heroism
Holiness	Honesty	Honor	Hopefulness
Hospitality	Humility	Humor	Hygiene
Imagination	Impact	Impartiality	Independence
Individuality	Industry	Influence	Ingenuity
Inquisitiveness	Insightfulness	Inspiration	Integrity
Intellect	Intelligence	Intensity	Intimacy
Intrepidness	Introspection	Introversion	Intuition
Intuitiveness	Inventiveness	Investing	Involvement
Joy	Judiciousness	Justice	Keenness
Kindness	Knowledge	Leadership	Learning
Liberation	Liberty	Lightness	Liveliness
Logic	Longevity	Love	Loyalty
Majesty	Making a difference	Marriage	Mastery
Maturity	Meaning	Meekness	Mellowness
Meticulousness	Mindfulness	Modesty	Motivation
Mysteriousness	Nature	Neatness	Nerve
Nonconformity	Obedience	Open-mindedness	Openness
Optimism	Order	Organization	Originality
Outdoors	Outlandishness	Outrageousness	Partnership
Patience	Passion	Peace	Perceptiveness
Perfection	Perkiness	Perseverance	Persistence
Persuasiveness	Philanthropy	Piety	Playfulness
Pleasantness	Pleasure	Poise	Popularity
Potency	Power	Practicality	Pragmatism
Precision	Preparedness	Presence	Pride
Privacy	Proactivity	Professionalism	Prosperity
Prudence	Punctuality	Purity	Rationality
Realism	Reason	Reasonableness	Recognition
Recreation	Refinement	Reflection	Relaxation
Reliability	Relief	Religiousness	Reputation

Resilience	Resolution	Resolve	Resourcefulness
Respect	Responsibility	Rest	Restraint
Reverence	Richness	Rigor	Sacredness
Sacrifice	Sagacity	Saintliness	Sanguinity
Satisfaction	Science	Security	Self-control
Selflessness	Self-reliance	Self-respect	Sensitivity
Sensuality	Serenity	Service	Sexiness
Sexuality	Sharing	Shrewdness	Significance
Silence	Silliness	Simplicity	Sincerity
Skillfulness	Solidarity	Solitude	Sophistication
Soundness	Speed	Spirit	Spirituality
Spontaneity	Spunk	Stability	Status
Stealth	Stillness	Strength	Structure
Success	Support	Supremacy	Surprise
Sympathy	Synergy	Teaching	Teamwork
Temperance	Thankfulness	Thoroughness	Thoughtfulness
Thrift	Tidiness	Timeliness	Traditionalism
Tranquility	Transcendence	Trust	Trustworthiness
Truth	Understanding	Unflappability	Uniqueness
Unity	Usefulness	Utility	Valor
Variety	Victory	Vigor	Virtue
Vision	Vitality	Vivacity	Volunteering
Warmheartedness	Warmth	Watchfulness	Wealth
Wholeheartedness	Willfulness	Willingness	Winning
Wisdom	Wittiness	Wonder	Worthiness
Youthfulness	Zeal		

Step Two: Cull & Transfer:

Grab your Post-its or notecards. Write down each of the values you circled on its own Post-it or card. As you're writing, narrow your list. Get all the notes where you can see them—a wall, board, or table.

Step Three: Sort & Title:

Look for patterns in your words and group similar ideas together. Maybe you put adventure, amazement, wonder, daring, and zeal in a group. Or perhaps pride, respect, power, and adoration fit together.

Once you have all the cards sorted into groups, pick one word from the group as the title. (You may remove a few more too.) For example, in adventure, amazement, wonder, daring, and zeal, you might choose daring as your title. If you have more than

5 groups, regroup until you have only 2-5. Once you've got the groups you like, keep all the cards in their groups.

Step Four: Select & Name

Now look at the titles. Does that set of titles feel unique to you? Or do those words feel like the same ones you see everywhere? Do you have a gut feeling of alignment?

You'll likely notice 2 of the values seem in tension with one another or a paradox of some kind. You want this. In *When More is Not Better*, management expert Roger Martin argues the complex nature of business requires integrative and adaptable thinking. These seemingly opposing values will force you to think creatively and move past oversimplifying complex realities.

Once you feel you've landed on the right 2-5 titles, those words are your values. But don't throw out any cards at this stage. You'll need those other words for the next step, Voicing your Values. List your 2-5 values here (the order isn't important right now.)

My core values:

Voice Your Values ⏱ *20-30 minutes*

Words without definitions are meaningless in practice. You need to define these values for yourself. The reason you chose those values might not be connected to the *Oxford English Dictionary* definition—and that's the point! Values are unique to you. To live by them, you must articulate what they mean *to you*.

Here you'll write your definitions. If you need some inspiration, read a dictionary definition or two to get you started. (Don't abdicate your thinking to ChatGPT or Claude.) Use the other words in the category to help you clarify your meaning.

This is first for you, not others. *You* must be able to define it for yourself. Don't get all Shakespeare or corporate structure speak. Write how you'd explain it to your best friend or a kindergartner.

Define the values you selected in your own words. Keep each definition to 1-2 sentences (I feel the struggle in my soul). But concise and clear is better than clever and convoluted. Start with the 1 that feels easiest.

Value:

Value:

Value:

Value:

Value:

Identify Meaning ⏱ *20-30 minutes*

If your values stay in this book, they aren't helpful. You need to integrate them into the way you think. Even though it's likely you've gone further than you've gone before, you're still on the way to use values to cultivate joy. So we're going back to story.

This exercise is tying your values to real life characteristics and experiences. Here's how to complete the chart:

Value: write 1 of your values.	**Definition:** write out your definition.	
Column One: **Aligned Actions** What do I do when I'm living out this value?	**Column Two:** **Misaligned Actions** What do I do when I'm not living this value?	**Column Three:** **Situations & Stories** When have I experienced this in real life?
Make a bulleted list of actions, behaviors, or examples that show you're living in alignment with that value.	List actions, behaviors, or examples that don't align with that value. Go with typical examples, not the extremes.	Find 1 experience or situation—1 story—that illustrates this value. Reminder: A story is 1 specific moment in time. It has a place, a time, characters—not a list of generalities. The more vivid and specific, the better. Think telling the story over dinner, not job description bullets.

Here's an example if your value is integrity.

Value: Integrity		
Definition: Integrity is being honest even when it's uncomfortable. It's trying to stay consistent in how I act and what I value. Being responsible for the consequences when I miss the mark, even when no one's watching.		
Column One: **Aligned Actions** What do I do when I'm living out this value?	**Column Two:** **Misaligned Actions** What do I do when I'm not living this value?	**Column Three:** **Situations & Stories** When I have experienced this in real life?
· Accurately track project hours · Keep confidences · Show up on time · Apologize · Make things right after mistakes	· Gossip · Blame · Pad an expense report · Break promises	I had been diligent about recording my hours for the project with Card Brand. One day, Phil in accounting came to me because Card Brand had complained about the number of hours they'd been billed on another job and asked for an audit of all their projects. I easily shared my records—with job numbers and times—feeling calm and confident about my work.

Complete this chart and repeat this process for each of your values (see the Fillable Frameworks for more or use your own paper.) You'll start to see connections among them and sometimes one story will highlight more than one value. Challenge yourself to write at least 1 story for every value.

Value:		
Definition:		
Column One: **Aligned Actions** What do I do when I'm living out this value?	**Column Two:** **Misaligned Actions** What do I do when I'm not living this value?	**Column Three:** **Situations & Stories** When have I experienced this in real life?

Guide by Rank ⏱ 5 *minutes*

Now it's time to rank your values in order of importance—for you, right now. This isn't permanent; revisit and reorder, and that's perfectly normal.

Think of this as creating a decision filter. When I was at business retreat at Disney, I learned their top value is *safety*. No matter how dazzling the show, if it isn't safe, they won't do it. That clarity builds trust in your decisions.

Remember: there is no wrong order. This is more clarity about how you want to cultivate joy.

Which value is your first filter—the one you'll always check before making a choice? What comes next, and then after that?

Guiding Questions:

- What's my deal-breaker value—the one I'll never compromise? (Start there!)
- Which value do I most want others to experience from me?
- Which value, if I ignore it, leads to regret?

1. _____
2. _____
3. _____
4. _____
5. _____

Activate and Integrate ⏱ 15-?? *minutes*

Your purpose grows from your values. Remember Jade Simmons' definition of purpose: "Purpose isn't what you do. It's what happens in other people when you do what you." If you want to live in alignment with your values and live into your purpose, then you need to make it all a part of your everyday life.

Write your purpose intention:

Here are 2 purpose mad libs to get you started. You can expand and revise your purpose intention as you live with it.

My purpose is to _____ with _____ so they _____.
                        verb type of person   skill/solution   result

I help to _____ by _____ so they can _____.
             type of person   solution   result

e.g.: My purpose is to equip parents with emotional and leadership skills, so they raise well-adjusted, emotionally healthy adults.

We all need reminders far more often than we think! Especially when something is new, you need to activate that new choice *and* integrate it into your life. This part of NAVIGATE is where you get creative!

Make them visible:
Write your purpose intentions and values down, post them somewhere you'll see often, or create a visual or verbal reminder that keeps them front of mind. *The goal is to make your values impossible to forget.*

A few ideas:

Some clients choose photographs or imagery that represent each value and display them. Others write on Post-it notes to keep on their desk. One even wrote a short jingle for every value!

Whatever helps *you* stay connected to your values is the right choice. Make sure your values—and their definitions—live somewhere visible. That means outside of your head. You want to *see/say/hear* them often enough, so they begin to guide your decisions automatically.

Transform and Evolve ⏱ *5-10 minutes*

At the start of an orchestra or band concert, from elementary gyms to Lincoln Center, the players tune their instruments. If a soloist comes out, they'll quickly tune again with the ensemble. Because one instrument playing on its own will eventually drift out of tune.

Transformation doesn't happen in a vacuum. Ever. You need other people to help you stay in alignment—or in tune—with your values. You need to build your Values Village.

Write the names of 2-3 people to share your values with. You're connecting with your people, but you're also inviting them to notice when your actions are (or are not) aligning with your values. Consider trusted friends, mentors, teammates, or boss.

Then, write when and how you'll contact them (phone call, text, email) to ask.

Pro tip: Include the year in your date. When you look back and revisit, it's helpful to know when you first talked with your Values Village.

Values Village

Name	When and how to ask

Here's a sample script:

Hey! I've been working on my making may values really clear. Can I share them with you? I'd love your help to notice when I'm living them and when I'm drifting off track.

Embody and Decide

The last step is ongoing. You now have incredibly clear values—with definitions, examples, stories, and a ranked order—plus your purpose and Values Village to help you live them out.

From here, your work is to *embody* those values in everyday decisions. Let them guide how you lead, relate, and choose what's next.

You'll use your values in chapter 8 on decisions and in chapter 10 in building structures. If you want more support with your values, I'd love to help you with coaching sessions or other experiences. For now, you've created your compass—one that helps you NAVIGATE a life that moves steadily toward joy.

The future of work and the center of joy is being more human.

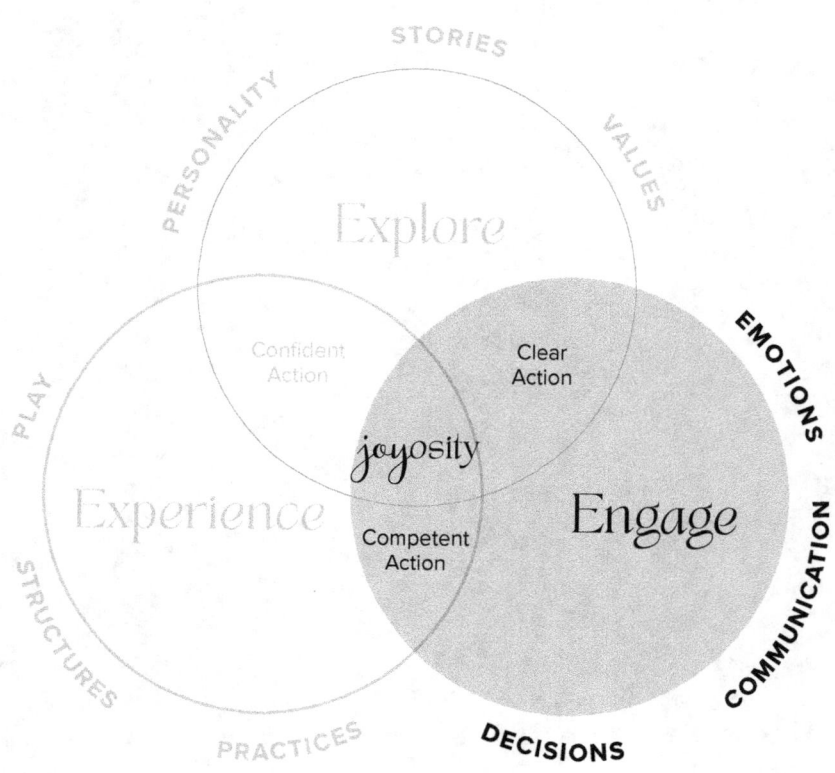

Part Two

Engage

People Power Skills

After you've explored internally, now it's time to build those People Power Skills you need to lead with joy. These exercises train you to engage with other people.

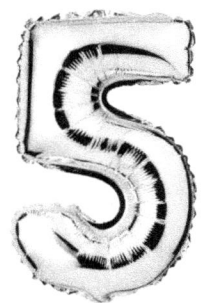

Your Emotional Fitness Drill

You don't want a workplace full of unnecessary drama, but you also don't want one so sterile that it's joyless. Repressing and recycling feelings kills connection.

The foundational skill of emotional intelligence is recognizing and managing your emotions first. If you recycle or repress them, you will be at the mercy of the tsunami or the dam that could burst at any time.

You must regulate yourself because you can't regulate anyone else! In *Joyosity* chapter 6, you learned the quick version of Name-Rate-Find. This is a more robust version to lead you to more nuanced emotional fluency.

Name-Rate-Find

Name the emotion/feeling. **Rate** its intensity. **Find** it in your body.

Name

After work one day, a few friends and I went out for a drink. Rain had left puddles everywhere. As we crossed the parking lot, an odd, sharp smell hung in the air. I was trying to place it when my friend London declared, "Ugh. It smells like old, wet boot!" I burst out laughing—because that was exactly it. Not a wet shoe, but *old, wet boot.*

Besides amusement, there was a satisfying feeling of clarity. And that's what you want with emotions too. Accurately labeling emotions and feelings reduces their intensity and that out-of-control feeling.

When you're experiencing an emotion you don't name, there is confusion and mild concern. That feeling of "What is that?" actually compounds and intensifies your emotional state. This process, called affect labeling, activates both logic and story in the brain, helping you regulate rather than react.

- Name the emotion with your out loud voice.
  When you use your voice for affect labeling, you engage your hippocampus and hypothalamus. You're literally moving the swirl of energy inside of you. Simultaneously declaring and hearing the data reinforces the information.

- Use the verbs "experience" or "feel."
  In English we don't have separate "to be" verbs to describe a permanent state versus a temporary state. This creates a lot of confusion around emotions and feelings. When we use "I am" it's easy to view emotions as permanent rather than temporary.

- Talk to yourself in the third person.
  Talk to yourself like a gentle friend or caring parent. This is another way to regulate the emotion and a relatively effortless form of self-control. Remember: gentle friend tone. Not scorn or shame!

Here's the sentence:

I feel [emotion/feeling]. Or I'm experiencing [emotion/feeling].

Remember from *Joyosity*, emotions are raw data and feelings have meaning added. Not good or bad, right or wrong. Dr. Susan David, Harvard psychologist and emotional expert writes, "The conventional view of emotions as good or bad, positive or negative is rigid. And rigidity in the face of complexity is toxic." So we use comfortable, unsure, and uncomfortable instead of binary judgements.

When you're experiencing emotions and feelings, your amygdala is sucking all the power to face the threat. Reduce the cognitive load by using the list. You may have feelings to add. The more you connect how you feel to specific names, the better your emotional fluency and self-awareness will be.

Feelings List

Comfortable Feelings	Inspired	Bored	Unsure	Inadequate
	Jolly	Bewildered	Uneasy	Insulted
	Joyful	Concerned	Vigilant	Isolated
Accepting	Jubilant	Confused	Worried	Jealous
Adored	Light-hearted	Cornered	**Uncomfortable Feelings**	Let down
Admiration	Lovable	Distracted		Livid
Adoration	Loving	Dread		Loathing
Affectionate	Motivated	Eager	Aggressive	Lonely
Amazed	Optimistic	Fearful	Angry	Mad
Amused	Outgoing	Frustrated	Anguished	Melancholy
Attraction	Passionate	Gob smacked	Ashamed	Miserable
Awe	Peaceful	Gloomy	Averse	Mortified
Cared for	Playful	Glum	Blue	Neglected
Cheerful	Pleasured	Guilty	Bitter	Offended
Comfortable	Proud	Hesitant	Contempt	Outraged
Confident	Raptured	Hysterical	Defeated	Pessimistic
Content	Relieved	Inadequate	Dejected	Rage
Curious	Respected	Interested	Depressed	Rejected
Dazzled	Satisfied	Insecure	Despondent	Resentful
Delighted	Secure	Irritated	Disappointed	Revolted
Desirable	Serenity	Longing	Discouraged	Sad
Determined	Silly	Lost	Disdain	Scornful
Eager	Thoughtful	Malaise	Disgusted	Shameful
Easygoing	Thrilled	Nervous	Dismayed	Sorrowful
Ecstatic	Triumphant	Overwhelmed	Despair	Spiteful
Elated	Trusting	Panicked	Distressed	Stupid
Encouraged	Valued	Pensive	Disregarded	Terror
Energetic	Wonderful	Pity	Doubtful	Tormented
Enthralled	Zealous	Resistant	Embarrassed	Unlovable
Enthusiastic	Zesty	Remorseful	Envious	Upset
Euphoric	**Unsure Feelings**	Self-conscious	Exasperated	Vengeful
Excited		Shocked	Foolish	Violated
Exhilarated		Skeptical	Forgotten	Worthless
Fascinated	Afraid	Startled	Furious	Wounded
Fond	Agitated	Stubborn	Grief	Woeful
Gentle	Aggravated	Surprised	Grouchy	Wrathful
Glad	Alarmed	Suspicious	Grumpy	
Glee	Alienated	Sympathetic	Helpless	
Goofy	Annoyed	Tense	Homesick	
Happy	Anticipation	Trapped	Hopeless	
Harmonious	Anxious	Uncomfortable	Horrified	
Helpful	Apprehensive	Unsafe	Humiliated	
Hopeful	Astonished		Hurt	

Rate

Emotions interconnect and vary in intensity. Emotional intensity increases when you are hungry, afraid, angry, lonely, or tired. It can depend on the literal weather, hormonal fluctuations, stress level, and personality structure.

> Ask yourself:
> How intensely am I feeling this emotion?

Don't overthink it. Literally, just feel it. You can use a color system from ultraviolet (low intensity) to infrared (high intensity). You can also use a number scale of 1 to 10. To avoid overthinking, it helps to actually touch the scale below.

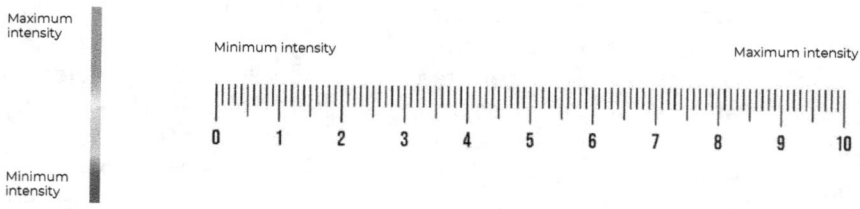

As you rate intensity, you'll also see how activated you are—the higher the intensity, the harder self-control becomes. When I guide clients and teams, I give this rule of thumb:

> Red Zone? Leave it alone.
> If it's a 7, wait a second.

At that intensity, ask for a pause. Step outside, take a walk, or simply breathe. Give the emotion space to move through you—otherwise, you'll face the very tsunami you're trying to avoid.

Enneagram Feels Wheel

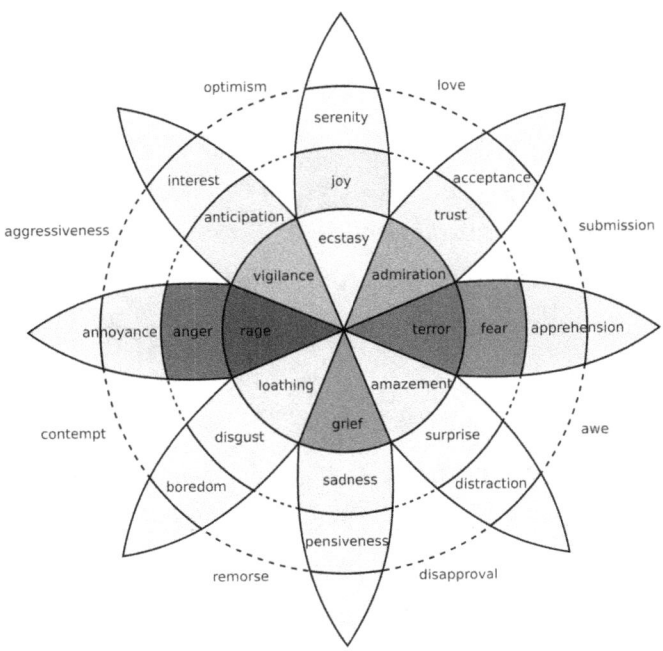

Dr. Robert Plutchik's Emotion Wheel gives you a way to see how core emotions connect and vary in intensity so you can spot the subtle shades of what you're really feeling. The wheel helps you notice the nuance between rage and annoyance or the blend of sadness and surprise that creates disapproval.

If you remember back in chapter 2, the different Enneagram groups share common emotional struggles.

Body Group: Eights, Nines, and Ones: Struggle with anger and control when belonging is threatened.

Heart Group: Twos, Threes, and Fours: Struggle with shame and grief when love is threatened.

Head Group: Fives, Sixes, and Sevens: Struggle with fear and isolation when safety is threatened.

As you practice emotional fluency combined with the Enneagram, you'll observe how your personality drives your feelings. Building on the work of Dr. Plutchik and Enneagram teacher Erin Slutsky, I designed the Enneagram Feels Wheel to be a bridge between your personality patterns and your emotional fluency.

How to Use the Wheel

Like the other name and rate tools, use this to label and process feelings with more nuance and accuracy.

- *The Center: Root Emotional Goals*

  The dark center holds the core emotional goals for each group: Belonging, Love, and Safety.

- *The Inner Rings: Feelings in the Goal*

  Feelings in the darker rings are in the same family as your emotional goal. These feelings mean you're experiencing more of your deepest desire and your favorite self.

- *The Outer Tabs: Core Emotional Struggles*

  The tabs around the circle name each group's default struggle: Anger & Control, Grief & Shame, Fear & Isolation. These appear when your fundamental fear is activated and your personality starts to take over.

- *The Outer Rings: Intensity and Activated*

  The lighter outer rings show variations in intensity of those core struggles.

Remember, everyone experiences anger, shame, and fear as much as everyone wants love, safety, and belonging. The Enneagram Feels Wheel helps you use your personality awareness to recognize your indicators of your core emotional struggle. You'll improve your emotional fluency, develop empathy for others, and compassion for yourself.

anger & control

nine

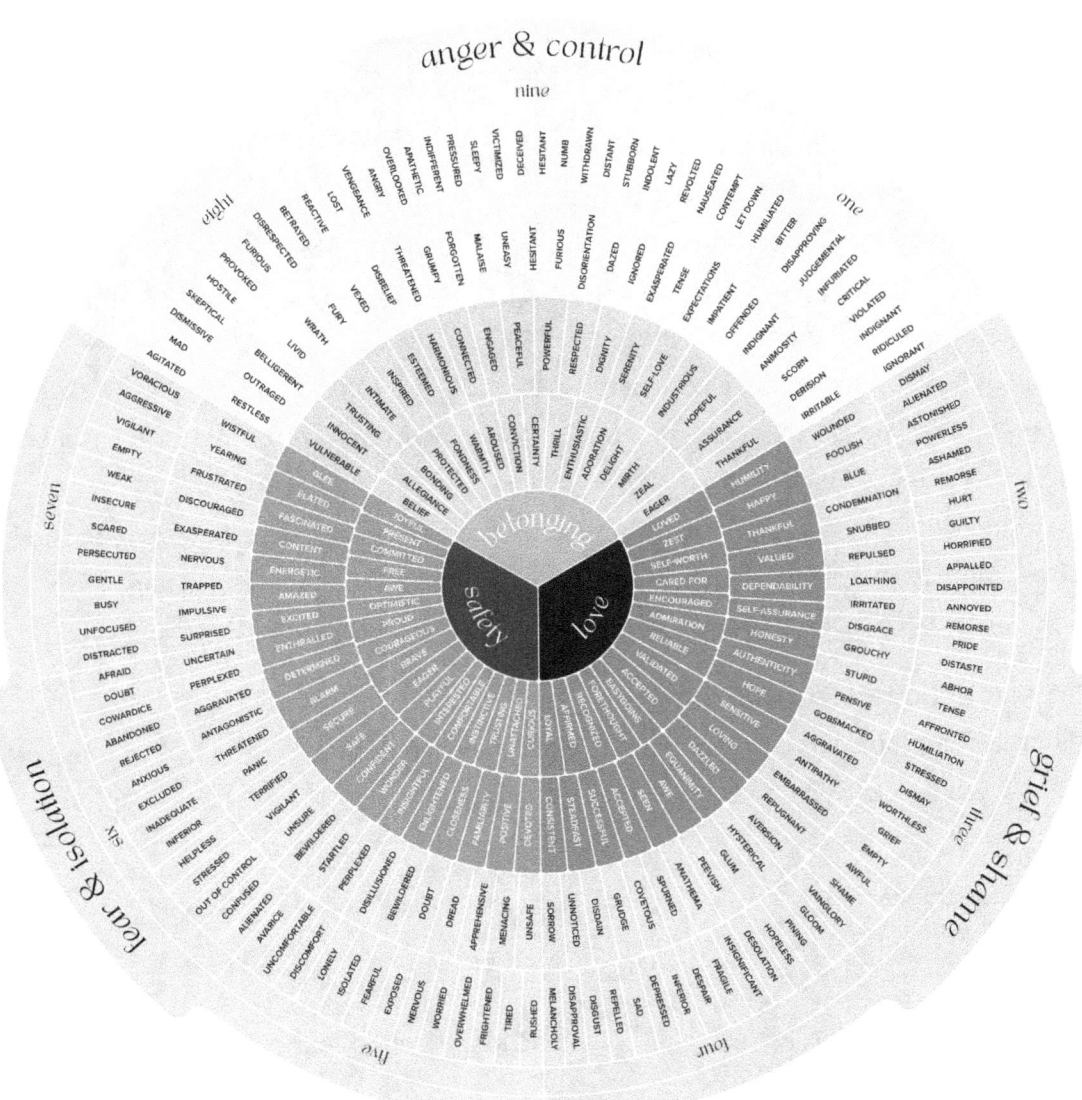

Find

Find trips up a lot of people. The physical sensations of emotions exist inside your very cells. Emotions are energy in motion, passing through as chemical reactions (You can check out all the research in *Joyosity*.). And many emotions have similar physical sensations. When you locate the emotions

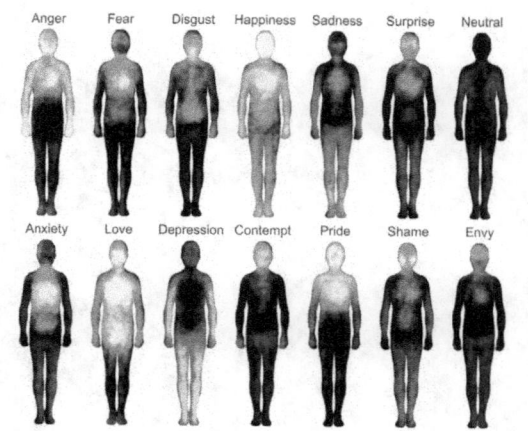

in your body, you get the executive lounge of your prefrontal cortex and the rest of your nervous system working together.

Researchers have mapped the typical patterns of where emotions show up in the body. The heat map shows how emotions activate various body locations. For example, fear and excitement both show up in the belly. The difference can be how you label the feeling.

Physical Locations of Emotions

For the head, shoulders, knees, and toes version, here are some places to look in your body to clue you in to the emotion:

Head:	Shoulders:
· *Eyes:* sadness · *Jaw:* anger · *Throat:* sadness	· *Back of the neck:* anger · *Shoulders:* anger, anxiety · *Collarbones/upper chest:* sadness
Chest:	Core:
· *Heart:* anger, pride, longing · *Ribs:* envy, surprise, anxiety	· *Spine/upper abdomen:* joy, love, disgust · *Belly:* fear, shame, excitement · *Lower belly/pelvis:* peace, creativity, energy

As you practice, you'll identify other sensations that are unique to you.

Breathe

Once you locate the emotion in your body, breathe. Breathe and appreciate the feeling. Imagine the emotion traveling through and leaving your body.

Vocalize

Vocalize the feeling—not talk about it like a conversation, but the sound of the feeling. Ask yourself, what sounds does this make? Is it a giggle or a moan? It'll feel all kinds of weird at first (and you probably want to be alone), but make the sound.

Out of Order?

As you practice Name-Rate-Find, the order matters less. The key is hitting all three areas.

You may remember the story from *Joyosity* of my missed opportunity with Sarajane Case, a fellow Enneagram expert. The disappointment felt massive and could have easily derailed my work.

The back of my jaw tingled like I'd eaten sour candy, and my chest collapsed. Tears pricked my eyes, and I plopped my forehead on my desk.

Because I'd been practicing emotional fluency for a bit, I started Name-Rate-Find with those sensations. It was extreme disappointment—the emotion I avoid the most. I used the Enneagram Feels Wheel to notice that I also felt trapped and yearning, classic struggles for an Enneagram Seven.

My Seven-self immediately wanted to reframe, repress, or run, but I chose to breathe and feel it all. And to my surprise, after 45 seconds or so, the feelings passed.

Try it out: ⏱ *5 minutes*

Use the list or wheels to name 1-3 emotions and feelings you have right now:

_____

Rate its intensity:

_____

Where is this emotion in my body? What does it sound like?

_____

BREATHE. Get curious.
What does this feeling reveal about what I need right now—love, safety, or belonging?

_____

_____

Is there anything else it shows?

_____

_____

What to Do with the Emotional Data

Once you've processed the emotions and feelings, you can use the information from your Feeling Center. The core emotions are signals. As a leader, you can use the wisdom of these emotions and their related intensity to guide your next step.

Anger:	Something isn't right and needs to change.
Fear:	Something is dangerous and needs to be known.
Grief:	Something important is lost or needs repair.
Joy:	Something is good and wonderful.
Disgust:	Something needs to be avoided or resolved.
Trust:	Something is appreciated and stable.
Love:	Something is valuable and connected.
Surprise:	Something is unexpected and needs a new examination.

Name-Rate-Find is the practice that puts you in charge of your responses and regulating yourself so you can bring your favorite self wherever you go.

Communication Clarity Calls

You surely remember this from chapter 7 in *Joyosity*: **The goal of communication is shared meaning.**

Why communication feels hard: Communication isn't merely a fact transfer—and it's not a Door-Dash, no contact delivery either. To create shared meaning you have to go back and forth, and it's far more complex than most leaders assume.

Communication involves a *sender, a message, a channel, a receiver, encoding, decoding, and noise* (internal/external disruption). Shared meaning is disrupted by everything from literal distractions (like loud airports) to psychological filters (like trauma, personality, or Enneagram type).

The CLEAN Framework for Effective Communication

Our practical method to reduce miscommunication and increase clarity, connection, and joy. Clear, Listen with Curiosity, Emotional Regulation, Absorbing Stories, Nonverbal Awareness. Each section has work for that skill—mix and match as needed.

Clear:

Be specific. "Fill in the dashboard" isn't enough. Paint a picture of what "done" looks like.

Paint Done

Start with the big idea and what you want.

There's always a reason why you want something accomplished. Start with that idea. Paint the picture of done with story and intention. As a Brené Brown puts it, paint done.

Paint with these questions.

When you are you are painting done, using Know-Feel-Do creates a clearer picture. Ask these questions for yourself and when clarifying with others. You can always come back to the question: *Can you paint done for me?*

KNOW
· Why does this matter or is needed?
· What information is needed?
· Where does that information live?
· Who can help with information or training?
· What tools/programs are needed?
· What is the level of priority?

FEEL
· What value does this show?
· What is the feel of the end result?
· What is the feeling of the user or client?

DO
· What are the steps to complete?
· Who is responsible for each step?
· What is the start date and the due date?
· Is this ongoing or one-time?

Expectations

Painting done brings clarity and establishes healthy expectations. As a reminder, expectations are:

- Spoken
- Agreed upon
- Reasonable and resourced

Painting done is spoken, but you still need agreement and enough resources. You can simply ask for agreement and whether this is reasonable. For even greater clarity, use Brown's TASC approach.

TASC

TASK: Who owns the task?

AUTHORITY: Do they have the authority to be held accountable?

SUCCESS: Are they set up for success (resources, timeline, paint done)?

CHECKLIST: Is there a checklist of what needs to happen to complete the task?

Here's your quick cheat sheet:

Paint Done:
T: Who owns the task?
A: Do they have authority?
S: Are they set up for success?
C: Is there a checklist?

Listen with curiosity:

Avoid assumptions. Remember Ted Lasso's dart game and Walt Witman's attributed wisdom: "Be curious, not judgmental."

Curiosity is interest in the gap in knowledge, understanding, or experience and becoming emotionally and intellectually invested in closing the gap through exploration. Curiosity is centered on the other person's experience, point of view, emotions, and understanding.

Curiosity is about exploration not destination.

Practicing curiosity:

- **Listen all the way to the end.** Take a breath before you respond or ask a question. And be what David Brooks calls a "loud listener." Add "oohs and aahs and wows and no's" with head nods and focused attention.

- **Reflect back what you heard.** Use your own words to paraphrase the information and reflect back emotions. "So you sent the email on time with all the information, but they said they didn't get it. How frustrating."
- **Ask open-ended questions.** These are great to have in your vocabulary.
  - Can you tell me more?
  - How did you respond?
  - What happened next?
  - How do you feel?
  - What support do you need?

Emotional Regulation:

Emotions aren't bad; they're signals. It's how we express them that matters. You don't want the tsunami. You want the canal. Tears and taking a break are okay. Yelling isn't. See chapter 5 in this *Playbook* for more!

Absorbing Stories:

Stories activate oxytocin, mirror neurons, and dopamine, helping others understand, trust, and remember. A story with emotion and detail is far more powerful than a timeline or data set.

Stories in CLEAN communication are not summaries. Neither are they multi-volume epics that leave people confused at the end. We've already talked some about stories in chapters 3 and 4, but here is a broader communication story framework for using a story to communicate clearly with others.

Good stories have **characters** people recognize, genuine **emotions**, a focus on one **moment in time**, specific **details**, and an **arc**.

Characters: Someone to root for, connect with, and care about. At least 1 single character to see in the story. It could be a person, a pet, even a peony. The story lives in a character.

Emotions: The feelings and emotions experienced by the character(s). They don't have to be over-the-top, just real and relatable. (Use the emotion tools from chapter 5 to help.)

Moment: The small moment that's the focus. Go really tiny on a specific moment in time or physical location. Rather than "waiting to hear back," it's "staring at the '...' bubble, waiting for the reply." Or "preparing to present to the client" becomes "standing next to the conference room screen, checking the slide."

Specific details: The more vivid, precise, and sensory the better. A setting that's detailed and specific actually creates more universal connection. If you're telling a story from the 90s, rather than a mobile phone in the car, use a bulky bag phone between the seats. Rather than sat down, plopped into the hard plastic chair. Smells, textures, colors... paint the details.

Arc: The journey of the story to a point.

ARC: Before › *POP* › Now

You need people on a journey to a point for your stories to create shared meaning.

- **Before:** the context that shows why they should care. Introduce your character and their *experience* of the pain or problem. Set the scene for how it was before.
- **POP:** the moment something happens. This is the catalyst to change. It can be a discovery, revelation, a decision, a clear action step. The character has popped the bubble of before to make room for something new because of the pop.
- **Now:** the experience after the pop. What is the character's life like now? What have they improved, what lesson learned, how they're stronger or wiser because of the pop.

How to Use the Story Frame

Use this story frame to sketch out a story. Great times to use stories: sharing feedback, casting vision, contextualizing data, or explaining a change.

Start at the top.

- *Character:* Who's in this story? You, a team member, a child?
- *Emotions:* What were they feeling? Keep it real, not melodramatic.
- *Moment:* Zoom in on one small, vivid point in time.
- *Details:* Add the sensory pieces—see, touch, hear, smell, taste.

Then move to arc.

- *Before:* Describe the way it was. What problem or pattern sets the stage?
- *POP:* Capture the exact moment something shifted—a realization, decision, or action.
- *Now:* Show what's true or possible today because of that pop.

This isn't script writing. This is the backbone for crafting short, memorable stories that help others see, feel, and understand your point.

Character	Emotions	Moment		Details

Before	POP	Now

Nonverbal Awareness:

Communication is 80–93% nonverbal. And humans will always believe the body over the words.

This means at best 1/5 of communication is your vocabulary. In the highest percentage, 55% is body language, and 38% is vocal quality or tone. Experts identify 10 methods of nonverbal communication.

1. Body messages
2. Facial expressions
3. Eye movements
4. Touch, which includes physical touch and digital haptics
5. Paralanguage, which includes tone, vocal quality, emphasis, accents, rate of speech, volume
6. Silence
7. Spatial proximity and territory
8. Artifacts such as color, clothing, hair/make-up style, jewelry
9. Scents and fragrances
10. Use of and orientation to time

It's vital to remember that nonverbal communication isn't universal or the same in every circumstance. Culture, experiences, and individual perspectives deeply influence how you interpret nonverbal communication. You can't reduce nonverbal communication to an isolated gesture, so it's helpful to think about nonverbal communication as five Cs.

- *Context*: Situation, location, and power dynamics change how nonverbal messages influence shared meaning.
- *Clusters*: A group of gestures is more reliable in accurately interpreting nonverbal cues.
- *Connection*: The intimacy and history of the people communicating changes meaning.
- *Consistency*: A repeated pattern of nonverbal communication may be an unconscious habit.
- *Culture*: What a thumbs up and head nod mean in one culture may mean something very different in another.

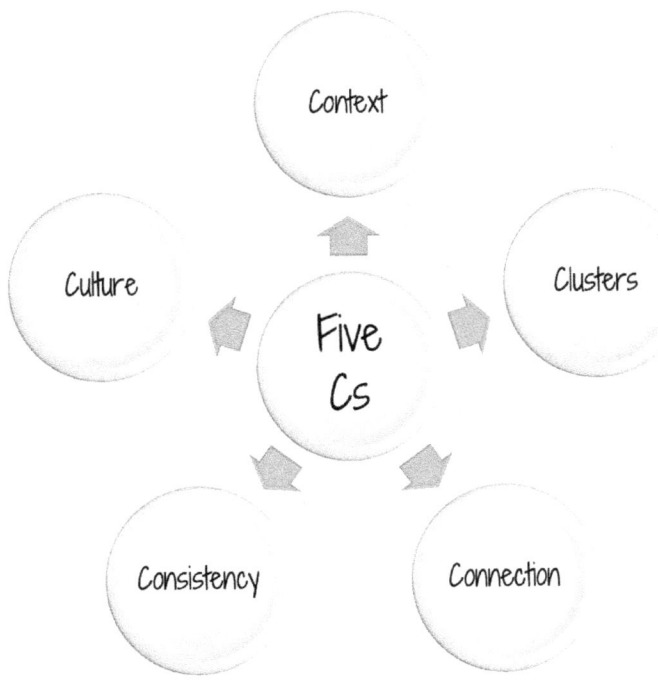

The Extra Mile: How to Improve your Nonverbal Communication

Nonverbal awareness is noticing the messages you're sending and reading others' messages with curiosity instead of assumption.

Choose one meeting or conversation to practice. Pick one that's fairly routine so you can devote energy to observing yourself.

Pick 1 from this list to be your focus. We're starting with the easiest ones. Over time, go through all 10.

Focus Nonverbal (Circle your focus)

Body messages	Facial expressions
Eye movements	Silence
Paralanguage—tone, vocal quality, emphasis, rate of speech, volume	Spatial proximity and territory

Describe this conversation:

Context:

_____

_____

Connection:

_____

_____

Culture:

_____

_____

During that time notice (Jot them down on paper—don't rely on memory.):

1. What are my nonverbals communicating?

2. What am I noticing from others?

After the meeting, review your notes and reflect:

Clusters: What did my nonverbals communicate as a group?

_____

_____

Clusters: What were the others' group of nonverbals?

_____

_____

Consistency: Is this a nonverbal habit for me?

Consistency: Do I notice these nonverbals in other people consistently?

Now what:
Is there anything I want to adjust?

How do I practice this?

Who else can I tell and have them reflect back to me what I'm working on?

CLEAN communication starts with awareness and ends with connection. Because the goal of communication is—say it with me now—shared meaning! And it's a practice. The best communicators are always working to improve their communication skills to cultivate the engagement that brings joy. If you want to bring this kind of clarity and connection to your team, I'd love to help.

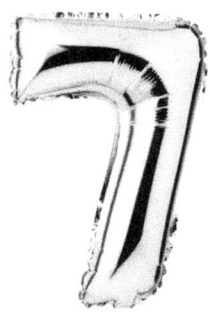

Keep Conflict In Bounds

Conflict is not inherently bad. It's a natural, necessary part of healthy relationships. And most of us hate it! Remember, **conflict is a struggle between limited resources and differing goals**, not a personal war with another person. *Joyosity* chapter 8 has the foundation, and we're building on that here.

LIMITED RESOURCES	DIFFERING GOALS
Time Money Space People	Love Safety Belonging

Conflict Styles

Your Enneagram personality has a lot to say when those core goals are threatened in a conflict. We're going to jump right in on ways for each type to improve in conflict situations.

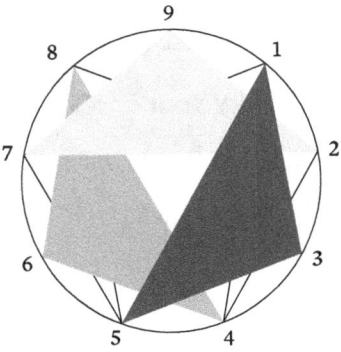

Below are descriptions of the *unhelpful conflict habits* that show up when that personality type is lit up. This isn't the type at their best—or all the time—but an honest picture of when conflict ignites the fundamental fear and other core motivations.

Developing Conflict Strategies: ⏱ *10 minutes*

Start with your type.

1. Identify your typical conflict sparks.
2. Label your go-to behaviors when that spark happens.
3. Answer the reflection questions. Use these questions on repeat to help you grow in conflict but also overall in cultivating joy.
4. Review the "Three Ways to Calm the Spark" at the end of this section. These actions are for every type.

Responding to other types in conflict: Each type includes a pro-tip for how you can respond to this type in conflict, meet them with understanding, and practice curiosity.

Dynamites

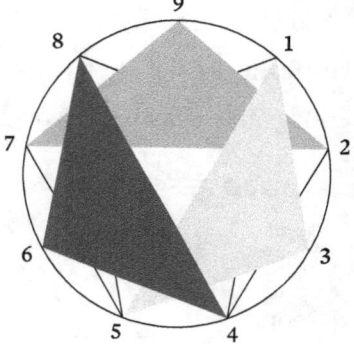

Enneagram Fours, Sixes, and Eights—Emotionally reactive and seek trust and validation.

Fours: See how hurt I am? No one feels like I do.

You can stir up conflict by being moody, self-absorbed, and unpredictable. You often react with high drama and internalize everything, blurring identity and emotion. Then, overwhelmed, you withdraw into imagination where problems can spiral into despair. And then creating solutions seems hopeless.

Identify your conflict sparks:

Which of these will spark your anger?

Being ignored · Asked to go aginst my values · Critique of my work · Envy comes up

Others?

What do you do when you feel that? What behaviors show up?

Reflection for Fours to grow in conflict:

What am I really angry about?
How am I focused on perceived rejection?
How am I stirring up unfair comparisons about myself?

Pro-tip for working with Fours:

Resist the urge to say, "Don't be so dramatic," or "You're overreacting."

Instead, curiously reflect back without reacting yourself. "This seems important to you. Are you feeling upset or frustrated?"

Sixes: Can I trust you to handle this? Can I even handle this?

You can stir up conflict by being pessimistic, skeptical, and jumping to worst-case scenarios. Because you're always scanning for danger, conflict can trigger your "I told you so" energy. That might explode into a rant, spiral into panic, or sink into self-doubt. And when you're unsure if you'll be blamed, resolving anything feels risky and unsafe.

Identify your conflict sparks:

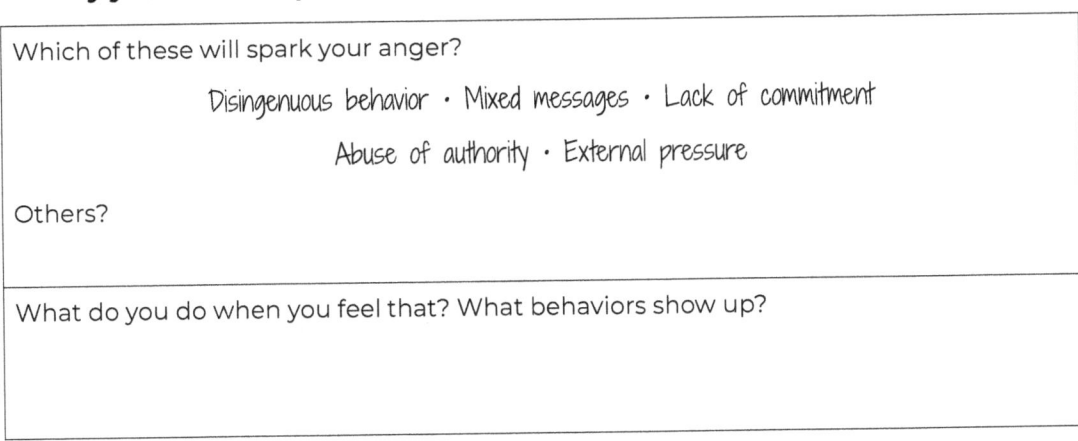

Which of these will spark your anger? Disingenuous behavior · Mixed messages · Lack of commitment Abuse of authority · External pressure Others?
What do you do when you feel that? What behaviors show up?

Reflection for Sixes to grow in conflict:

What am I getting from worse-case scenario planning?
How does my need for loyalty or my tendency to project my thoughts and feelings on others protect me from facing my own fears and feelings?
How could I grow if I practiced trusting myself?

Pro-tip for working with Sixes:

Resist the urge to say, "That will never happen," or "That's absurd."

Instead, kindly ask, "That's a big concern. How likely do you think that might be?" or "I can tell you're concerned. Let me clarify..."

Eights: I'm not shouting. I just want you to hear how mad I am.

You're not afraid of conflict. In fact, you kinda thrive on it. But your intensity, defiance, or contrarian streak can escalate it quickly. You speak your mind without a filter—but you're mistaking raw emotion for candor. You crave the realness of conflict because it reinforces your identity of strength and sense of belonging. Although you're quick to confront, you keep your guard up to protect your tender heart. And when vulnerability stays hidden, real resolution slips out of reach.

Identify your conflict sparks:

Which of these will spark your anger? Feeling blindsided · Shirking · responsibility · Avoiding the issue · Injustice · Dishonesty Others?
What do you do when you feel that? What behaviors show up?

Reflection for Eights to grow in conflict:

When do I intentionally try to intimidate someone? What's my purpose?
What do my strong reactions show me about my fears?
How could relaxing my grip on power help bring out my favorite self and more joy?

Pro-tip for working with Eights:

Resist the urge to say, "Who put you in charge?" or "You're being too much."

Instead, stand confident, strong, and calm. Say, "Your reaction is intense right now. Tell me more about why this is important to you."

Cool Cucumbers

Enneagram Ones, Threes, and Fives—Detach and prioritize logic while seeking feeling successful and competent.

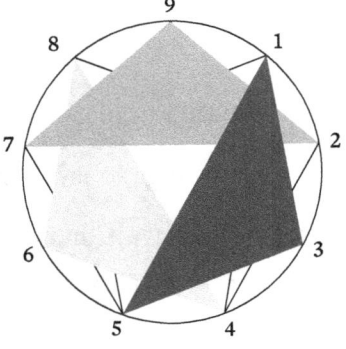

One: Let's be adults here. (I'm holding it together—why can't you?)

You can march yourself into conflict with impatience, rigidity, and a sharp eye for what's right. You might "per my last email" or "it's in the policy" in the name of justice and order. Believing that your principles and rules will lead to fair solutions, you contain your emotions to stay above their influence. The problem? Others can see you as cold or hypercritical—because they can't hear the inner critic already yelling at you "Failure!" And when people don't feel understood, trust breaks down and resolution stalls.

Identify your conflict sparks:

> Which of these will spark your anger?
>
> Criticism · Changing plans without collaboration · Lack of follow-through
> Deception · Rule-breaking · Being late
>
> Others?

> What do you do when you feel that? What behaviors show up?

Reflection for Ones to grow in conflict:

> What is the real source of my anger?

> Who are 3 people I respect? How might they perceive this situation? What could I learn from them?

> How could finding more than one way to be right soften my self-criticism?

Pro-tip for working with Ones:

Resist the urge to say, "You're so critical," or "You don't always have to be right."

Instead, ask with kind curiosity, "I wonder if there are other good options. What do you think?"

Three: I've got this handled. Just follow me, and I'll win.

Your competitive streak can pull you into conflict as much as arrogance or insincerity. Your efficiency machine—usually your superpower in crushing goals—becomes a stumbling block when emotions enter the conflict (which they always do). You sense how others feel, but your own emotions get shoved way down. People may feel your pragmatism to get it done matters more than they do. So you scheme, shortcut, and hustle through the messy parts to get through this construction zone slowing you down. But when you cut too many corners, you don't have a foundation for real resolution, and you miss the goal you were chasing in the first place.

Identify your conflict sparks:

Which of these will spark your anger?

Not looking good in front of others · Blamed for others shoddy work · Not getting credit
Feeling set up to fail · Illogical inefficiency · Effort feels uneven

Others?

What do you do when you feel that? What behaviors show up?

Reflection for Threes to grow in conflict:

What does appearing successful protect me from?

How do others' actions influence how I feel about my own success or failure? How do I respond when I feel competitive?

What could I gain if I focused less on impressing other people?

Pro-tip for working with Threes:

Resist the urge to say, "You don't always have to win," or "You're embarrassing yourself."

Instead, try asking, "How can we collaborate so we all succeed?"

Five: I need time to go into my mind castle. Too many feelings. Not enough data.

You weren't even trying to engage in conflict... and yet, you land in it by being too detached, isolated, or intellectually provocative. You crave objectivity and trust your knowledge and mental resources to solve problems. (Honestly, why can't others just stick to the facts?)

But when you emotionally detach, you miss the deeper wisdom inside you—and from others. You prefer to withdraw and think it through, but that often drags out conflict or turns it into a solo mission. You emerge from the Ivory Tower with a decree. Even when your solution is brilliant, doing it solo means others don't buy in. And you're left wondering if you missed something, or worse, if you're not as competent as you thought.

Identify your conflict sparks:

Which of these will spark your anger?
Lack of integrity · Taken off guard · Someone sharing your private information Overwhelming tasks · Pressure to emotionally respond · Feeling incompetent Others?
What do you do when you feel that? What behaviors show up?

Reflection for Fives to grow in conflict:

How might other people perceive my reactions (even if I don't see them like that)?
How do I separate from my emotions? How does that cause issues?
How could I engage if I believed people didn't deplete my energy, but could give to me?

Pro-tip for working with Fives:

Resist the urge to say, "Just decide already." or "That information doesn't matter."

Instead, curiously ask, "What information would help you to move forward?"

Silver Linings

Enneagram Twos, Sevens, and Nines—Choose optimism or denial to avoid discomfort and conflict

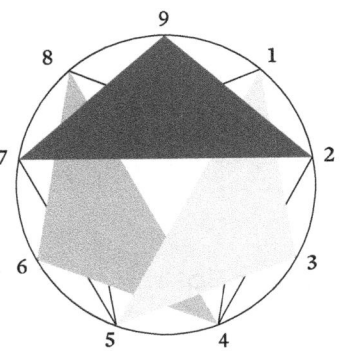

Two: Let me help you with your problem. Because I am not the drama. Right?

You get into conflicts by being too clingy, worried, or self-important. You tend to focus on your great qualities and all you did to help. (All while repressing your negative thoughts and feelings.) You desperately cling to the idea that your good intentions will earn you regard and approval. And with your grip so tight, you strangle honest, healthy conflict. Conflict feels like a threat to your love and identity. So you avoid the real issue and try to appease the other person to keep the peace. But in doing so, you enable or extend the conflict, pushing resolution further out of reach.

Identify your conflict sparks:

Which of these will spark your anger?

Inconsiderate, rude, or abusive behavior · Taken for granted · Lack of appreciation · Entitlement · Ignored input · Brusque or gruff communication

Others?

What do you do when you feel that? What behaviors show up?

Reflection for Twos to grow in conflict:

What does gratitude or direct appreciation for my work do for me?

How do I try to shape others' feelings and actions to keep their approval?

What could happen if didn't need to be liked?

Pro-tip for working with Twos:

Resist the urge to say, "You're smothering," or "You don't need to fix everything."

Instead, try asking, "I appreciate your willingness to help. Here's what would help most right now," or "What do you need right now?"

Seven: Not my circus. I'm on tour with merrier monkeys.

You drop into conflict by being impatient, irresponsible, and dismissive. Your go-to move? "Well, at least..." That instant reframe helps you dodge discomfort, but it also denies the truth that there is a problem.

You either parachute out or distract with "good vibes only" tactics: charm, jokes, or full-court press persuasion. Because you reframe in real time, you can walk away thinking nothing happened. Meanwhile, everyone else still sits in a mess. You have an incredible ability to see hopeful possibilities and create options, but you want the *movie montage* version of resolution, not the real work: taking responsibility, sitting with pain, or actually considering others' perspectives (because—ugh—that's such a bummer).

But here's the knife twist: if you avoid problems, the pain multiplies. And no matter how fast you spin it, you can only reframe so many times until you're left with a pale, copycat version of connection that looks shiny but pops like a bubble.

Identify your conflict sparks:

Which of these will spark your anger?

Micromanagement · Unjust criticism · Ignored ideas · Boring, tedious, or mundane tasks · Illogical negative emotions · Not taken seriously · Lack of options

Others?

What do you do when you feel that? What behaviors show up?

Reflection for Sevens to grow in conflict:

What does real-time reframing do for me? What am I avoiding or protecting?

How can I sit with negative experiences or feelings a bit longer?
What might open up if I felt uncomfortable emotions rather than distracting, reframing, or intellectualizing them?

Pro-tip for working with Sevens:

Resist the urge to say, "That's just how it is." or "Don't be naïve."

Instead, try asking, "I see you're frustrated. This reality isn't ideal. What solutions can you agree to that are still energizing to you?"

Nine: Nope. No conflict here. (Dear Reader, conflict? Everywhere.)

You avoid conflict at every turn but still manage to smack right into it with your indecision, disengagement, and good old-fashioned stubbornness. You focus on connection and harmony, and conflict feels like a threat to your U.N.-level peacekeeping efforts. "Can't we keep it like it is and get along? Is it really that big of a deal?" (Which you may or may not say out loud.) You believe things will work out on their own, but the truth is, the sand covers your head. And every grain is someone else's need you agreed to in the moment, just to keep the peace. Eventually, though, you feel unheard, overlooked, and resentful. And here's the kicker: it takes way more energy to maintain fake peace than it does to build real peace by addressing the conflict.

Identify your conflict sparks:

Which of these will spark your anger?
Feeling ignored · Hostility or rudeness · Taken advantage of · Lack of support · Unexpected, direct confrontation · Disruption of harmony · Being ordered or dictated to
Others?
What do you do when you feel that? What behaviors show up?

Reflection for Nines to grow in conflict:

What does self-forgetting—going with the flow or merging with others' ideas—give me? What am I avoiding?
How do I signal "yes" when I really mean "no"?
What could happen if saw conflict as a path toward connection?

Pro-tip for working with Nines:

Resist the urge to say, "Just decide already." or "Will you hurry up?"

Instead, with patience and curiosity ask, "How much time do you need to decide? Would this timeframe work?"

Three Ways to Calm the Spark

Every single type can do these steps:

1. Share your typical sparks at the beginning of a working relationship.
   "I find it helpful when..." "I tend to work best when..."

2. When you notice your spark behaviors show up, take a break and do something physical. Go for a walk, workout, or microbursts of intense activity.

3. Express your frustration as soon as you feel the spark but in a constructive way. You may need to ask for a break and set a time to come back to the conversation. Not one time have I regretted a pause.
   "I'm feeling frustration right now because..."
   "I want to make sure this stays productive. I'd like to take a break. Can we revisit this at [name a time.]

Smoothing Tricky Conversations

In *Joyosity* chapter 8, you learned when it's time to speak up and have the conversation: if harm is present, there is a break in relationship, or the behavior keeps repeating.

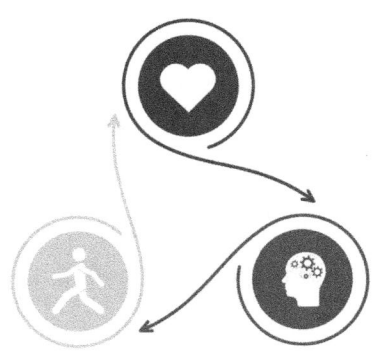

When it's time to have the tricky conversation, the Three Question Model gives you important data points in solving conflict.

The 3 questions areas:

1. How do you *feel*?
2. What do you *think*?
3. What do you want to *do*?

In the middle of difficult conversations, you must do more than hear. Hearing is important but still passive.

Active listening means attending to the sender, seeking to understand, connecting, remembering, and responding to the message. This is so much more than waiting for your turn to talk or crafting your rebuttal while the sender is talking.

In addition to your nonverbal messages, your words can smooth the path to problem-solving and shared meaning or create a crater that damages trust and prevents connection.

Conversational Gliders

Gliders are phrases and words that may feel awkward at first, but they glide the conversation forward.

Kind Opening

Getting started is often the most intimidating. Try these gliders.

- Can we talk?
- I am struggling with something, and I'd like to talk with you about it.
- I feel like something is off between us. Is there anything I've done you'd like to talk about?
- I made a mistake, and I'd like to talk with you about it.

- I'm feeling _____ by something that happened. Can we talk?
- I care about you and our relationship. Because you are important to me, I want to share an observation.
- Do you have time now or would another time be better?

Messy Middle

The messy middle can feel like a pothole-filled road to shared meaning. With all the back and forth, emotional regulation, deep listening, it's easy to get off track. In addition to your feel, think, do questions that you use on repeat, these questions illicit *micro-agreements*. The micro-yesses keep you and your conversational partner focused, engaged, and open.

- Can you say it again? I want to make sure I understand.
- Here's what I hear you saying ... (repeat back what they're saying). Is that right?
- Can I clarify something?
- Here's what I remember happening...
- Here's the story I'm telling myself right now...
- Yes, I see that. And... (not *but*)
- Can you say more words?
- Would you tell me more?
- Would you be open to a different perspective?

Connected Close

Once you've moved into shared meaning, chosen solutions and resolutions, these phrases help you *close the loop*. Open loops aren't full resolutions. There are lingering emotions and assumptions that will easily expand into a continued conflict and everyone feeling like *Why do we keep having this same fight?*

- Is there anything you need to say you didn't get to say?
- Is there anything you haven't heard you still need to hear?
- Have I answered all your questions?
- How can we work together to make a plan?
- Do you feel like we've resolved this issue?
- Thank you for listening to my perspective.
- Are we ok?
- I apologize.
- I forgive you.

Pro Tip: Especially if you are the leader or the one with more positional power in the situation, set the follow-up meeting right then. ESPECIALLY if someone has been brave enough to confront you, they've already risked a lot. Don't make them do it again. "Let's set a meeting for [appropriate amount of time] to check in." Open those calendars and set the meeting. You have built in accountability without the side of awkward trying to ask for another conversation.

Conversational Grenades

As the gliders improve communication and conflict resolution, these phrases will explode right in the middle of your problem-solving and break more trust. Remove these grenades and replace them with gliders.

Why?

I LOVE a good why question. But in a tense conversation, *why* puts folks on the defensive. Simply replace *why* with *what*.

- What are the reasons you...?
- What led you to that conclusion?

Always and Never

When you say, "You always..." or "You never..." you've set up an escape route that feels like an attack to the other person. Now they remember THE ONE TIME that disproved your statement, and nothing is resolved. Instead, try:

- Often, I see this happen...
- This is an issue sometimes...
- Many times...
- It's atypical...
- Rarely...

This is exactly what happened.

I have news—you remember "exactly what happened" differently than others. Your mind is not a video recorder. You create a story from an experience that becomes your memory. The story may be accurate, but not exact. The other person in the conflict will have a different story. Of course, there are observable facts, but facts only make sense in context.

How you make sense of the memory is important to the conversation, but saying it's "exactly what happened" allows the other person to dismiss your statement, halting the resolution process. Instead, try:

- What I remember is... How do you remember it?
- From what I wrote down, I remember...
- When I looked back through the notes, I discovered...
- From what I recall...
- Here's the story as I remember it...

Stop being emotional!

A truly impossible ask! As we've discussed, emotions indicate important data points. So you need them. Instead, try:

- This conversation feels intense. I need to take a breath.
- I'm feeling elevated and having a hard time being in control.
- Can we pause? I'm feeling like this is getting out of hand. Let's come back in 15 minutes.
- I feel like you are shouting at me. Please stop.
- Can you help me understand why you feel that way?
- What are some reasons you feel like that?

I-Statements

These little statements can feel counterintuitive. Aren't you supposed focus on listening to the other person? Yes, and...when it is your time to express your perspective, if you start with "You do..." it's a poke in the chest. Instead, I-statements show you taking responsibility for your own emotions, perspectives, and requests.

SENTENCE STARTER	CONTENT
I feel...	Emotion
When you do/don't do/this happens...	Specific situation
Because I think it means...	Why you care, the story you're telling yourself
I'd like...	What you want
Would you consider...	Specific Action

It can sound like this:

I feel taken advantage of when you leave the toaster out and crumbs on the counter. Because I think it means I'm the one that has to clean it up and that you think you don't have to be responsible for our shared space. I'd like the counter to be clear. Would you consider putting the toaster away and giving the counter a quick wipe?

Use the chart to prepare I-statements. As you practice, you'll naturally start to adopt this vocabulary.

The Lock and Dam Stages of Conflict

Wind whipping around, the smell of the lake, and the expanse of Lake Michigan—the Chicago Wendella River Boat never gets old for me. It's a beautiful few hours on the water.

The part that always tests everyone's patience? Going from the Chicago River to Lake Michigan. The boat must pass through a lock and dam system to leave the river onto the lake and then return back to the city. The slow system is a series of connected "tubs" or locks that slowly fill with water to lift the boat to the next level. Then dam for the boat to move forward. And repeat.

True interpersonal conflict resolution is much like that process. A boat cannot leap from the Chicago River out to Lake Michigan, and you cannot collapse the lock-and-dam system of resolution into one conversation.

There are 4 distinct stages of conflict resolution. You can move through them quickly, but if you try to skip a lock, you will end up with more problems. The 4 locks of resolution are

1. Responsibility and Release
2. Reconcile and Resolve
3. Rebuild and Restore
4. Reinstate and Reintegrate

Four Locks of Resolution

Responsibility & Release   Reconcile & Resolve   Rebuild & Restore   Reinstate & Reintegrate

Responsibility and Release

In this stage, you own your role in a conflict. Rarely is a conflict 50/50. Sometimes it's 94/6. Even if your part is 6%, you are 100% responsible for your 6%. And you make amends for your part.

Internally, you release the other person by choosing not to hold this against them anymore. You release yourself from resentment and dwelling on the incident. As much as we want an apology, or even acknowledgement, from other people, you can release someone without it.

In some cases, you won't move on to the next stage. Releasing or forgiving doesn't mean you have an ongoing relationship. There are more steps to get there.

Reconcile and Resolve

This stage is mutual ownership of the struggle and working for creative solutions to resolve the conflict. Reconciliation includes restitution or "making it right." Together, you make a plan of interaction moving forward.

Rebuild and Restore

My parents always talked about the trust bank. When you break trust, you withdraw from the bank. This stage is making consistent deposits into the trust bank.

NOTE: Sometimes all the trust has been rebuilt, but a new incident like the original happens. You must go back to Responsibility and Release because now someone has broken a new commitment they made in Reconcile and Resolve. That's not dwelling on it or bringing it back up again. This is a new issue to resolve.

This stage is longer than most of us like. You are rebuilding trust and respect. You are following through with the plan and restitution you agreed to in the previous step.

Reinstate and Reintegrate

Some actions and offenses require removing someone from a position or setting stronger boundaries about how you interact together until you've moved through Rebuild and Restore.

Reinstating grants someone's previous level of access or relationship. Reintegrating establishes a new way of working together.

NOTE: There are some offenses that disqualify a person from reinstatement into a specific role or around certain people. For example, embezzlement, physical violence, abuse, or harassment.

When you avoid conflict, you manufacture fake peace. Use these tools to turn conflict into connection. These aren't all the strategies I use with clients, but they're what you need to notice your sparks, practice curiosity, and close the loop in conflict so you build trust and joy.

Make the Wise Call

These additional tools complement and expand on chapter 9 in *Joyosity*, helping you make wise decisions. Remember, the process of making decisions is more important than the decision itself. With a wise process you make informed choices, growing resilient joy—regardless of the outcomes.

When your values align with your company's purpose, you're 53% more satisfied with your job than if you're misaligned.

Who's Making the Decision

You want to start with knowing your Enneagram Leadership Style—Trailblazer, Connector, or Professor—from *Joyosity* and the NAVIGATE process from chapter 4. Use the ranked values when making decisions.

The Personal Board

You only have your knowledge, experience, and perspective. Gathering a group expands what Annie Duke calls the ability to "test alternative hypotheses and move toward accuracy." You need a Personal Board with different voices for different areas of your life. Building a board before you need it gives you wisdom on call.

Create your Personal Board of 5 to 12 mentors, sponsors, coaches, and peers—wise friends, advisors, cheerleaders, and straight-shooters. Aim for a diverse group of genders, races, and experiences as well as people inside and outside your industry,

Mentors walk just ahead of you, offering perspective on what you haven't experienced. They help you see up around the bend, what you can't see because you haven't been there yet.

Sponsors promote you and mention you in rooms you aren't in yet. They open doors of opportunity and expand your imagination of what's possible, like a bridge across a cavern.

Coaches help you interpret what you already know (I include therapists and spiritual directors in this group.). They ask great questions to help you develop wisdom, self-awareness, clarity, and goals—part mirror, part map.

Peers walk with you. At a similar stage of life or career, they notice what you may have forgotten because they've watched you grow. They remind you of past lessons or wins. Newer peers commiserate and offer "here's what's working for me right now," because they're walking the same stretch of road.

Each person on your board brings the energy of one (or more) of these support styles:

Challengers push you to face reality, bring clarity, and say what needs to be said—even if it stings.

Cheerleaders remind you who you are, your values your capabilities, and encourage you to keep going.

Connectors build bridges to people or resources, introducing you and lending their credibility.

Developing Your Personal Board ⏱ *60-90 minutes*

Step One: Brainstorm the Board ⏱ *10-15 minutes*

1. Brainstorm 3 to 5 names for each role. Choose people you know first. Then add at least 1 Guiding Voice—someone who fills the role through their example or work, even if you don't know them yet. Some of my Guiding Voices have become true board members and friends.
2. Circle the support style(s) that fits them best.

MENTORS	
Name:	Challenger · Cheerleader · Connector
Name:	Challenger · Cheerleader · Connector
Name:	Challenger · Cheerleader · Connector
Name:	Challenger · Cheerleader · Connector
Name:	Challenger · Cheerleader · Connector
Guiding Voice:	Challenger · Cheerleader · Connector

SPONSORS	
Name:	Challenger · Cheerleader · Connector
Name:	Challenger · Cheerleader · Connector
Name:	Challenger · Cheerleader · Connector
Name:	Challenger · Cheerleader · Connector
Name:	Challenger · Cheerleader · Connector
Guiding Voice:	Challenger · Cheerleader · Connector

COACHES	
Name:	Challenger · Cheerleader · Connector
Name:	Challenger · Cheerleader · Connector
Name:	Challenger · Cheerleader · Connector
Name:	Challenger · Cheerleader · Connector
Name:	Challenger · Cheerleader · Connector
Guiding Voice:	Challenger · Cheerleader · Connector

PEERS	
Name:	Challenger · Cheerleader · Connector
Name:	Challenger · Cheerleader · Connector
Name:	Challenger · Cheerleader · Connector
Name:	Challenger · Cheerleader · Connector
Name:	Challenger · Cheerleader · Connector
Guiding Voice:	Challenger · Cheerleader · Connector

3. Review your list of names. Do you have each role and support style covered? If not, go back and add names.

4. Star the people you feel the most comfortable asking—not if you think they'll say yes or not! Do you still have each role and support style covered?

Step Two: Invite the Board ⏱ 20-30 *minutes*

Now that you've identified who fits each role and which support styles they bring, it's time to actually bring them on board. You want everyone to know you're building a personal board to help you make wise decisions, be a better leader, and cultivate more joy.

Here's how you can approach each type of person:

Mentors:

"Hey, I'm asking a few trusted mentors to help guide me. I'd love to check in with you every [time frame] and get your perspective as I navigate challenges and choices. Would you be interested?"

Sponsors:

"I'm building a personal board, and I see you as someone who really creates opportunities for others. Would you be willing to be what I call a sponsor? Someone who can occasionally help me connect with new opportunities or people?"

Coaches:

If you already have a coach, great! If not, consider what kind of coaching or support you need—like a leadership coach, business coach, or therapist. This will typically be someone in your organization, or you hire.

Peers:

Peers might need a friendly heads-up.

"I'm putting together a group of folks I can bounce ideas off of and check in with to help me when I'm making decisions or it's hard. Like my own personal board. Would you be one of those people?"

Note about Guiding Voices: You're not asking these people, but you can send them a thank you note sharing what their influence has meant to you.

Step Three: Record the Board ⏱ 5-10 minutes

Once you've had these conversations, you've established your Personal Board. Map your board here by filling in their names. Put it where you can see it (digitally or physically).

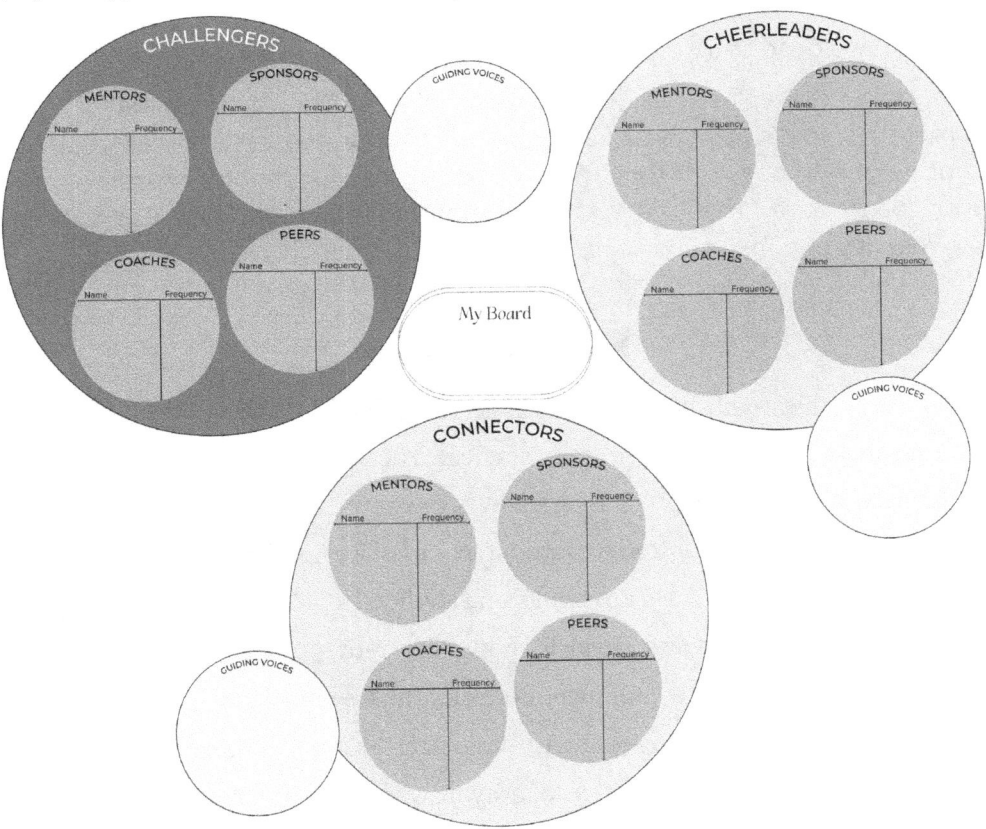

Step Four: Activate the Board ⏱ 20-30 minutes and ongoing

Once you've built the board, you've got to keep it alive if you want to create joy with your board.

Create a Personal Board Journal.

Not everyone tracks relationships the same way. Pick a tool that fits your personality and workflow. You can use visual builders and task trackers like Notion, Trello, ClickUp, or Asana. Simple spreadsheets like Google Sheets or Excel work great. Or if you prefer, use more robust relationship managers such as Dex or Cloze.

In the Appendix B, there's a table you can fill in. In the online resources, I've created a Google and Notion template for you. Whatever tool you choose, the goal is the same: stay intentional about connection, reflection, and growth.

Step Five: Reevaluate the Board

At least once a year, revisit the Board members. Ask yourself (and them) these questions:

1. Is this helping me?
2. Are we able to maintain this commitment?
3. Do we need to adjust expectations?

If the answers aren't yesses, your relationship isn't over. You simply shift. I get that sometimes, that's not practical. Maybe one of your peers was a walking buddy in your neighborhood, and they move out of town. Your mentor moves companies. Your coach retires. That's ok. You may simply lose touch naturally. But clear is kind, so when it's possible, make it clear.

Being a Wanter

In *Joyosity*, you learned about Dan Sullivan's Needers and Wanters.

Needers make decisions from scarcity and fear. They compete for limited resources, focus on security, and are typically reactive, anxious, or swayed by guilt and "shoulds." Needers make fear-based decisions that lead to burnout, poor choices, and compromises of integrity.

Wanters make decisions from possibility and abundance. They collaborate, imagine new futures, and act from values and intrinsic motivation rather than fear. Wanters make values-based decisions that lead to creativity, cooperation, freedom, and, of course, joy.

If you were conditioned to ignore what you want—to see wanting as selfish, risky, or unrealistic—you're likely out of practice identifying what you want. And then what you want seems out of reach.

If you find yourself unsure of what you want, here are a couple ways to uncover what you want and practice getting comfortable with being a Wanter.

NOTE: Shame will scream its way in here. Allow yourself to discover what you want with these activities without judging it. If you find yourself editing so it appears palatable to others, minimizing, or dismissing, try again. Sounds like: That's dumb. It's bad that I want that. That's crazy. Remember wanting is about direction in the process, not the decision.

Ask and Wait

I know this sounds basic, but we often rush past naming the want, assuming we know. You can do this out loud or on paper. Ask yourself and then wait for 10-20 seconds for the answer to come.

- What do I want?
- Is that what I really want?
- Is there anything else I want?
- If I could have anything, what do I want?

Ask and Walk

Go on a walk without headphones (I know. Appalling.) Before you go, ask yourself the questions above. On the walk, allow your mind to wander in your neighborhood or a park. Look at the sky, listen to the birds, wave to your neighbors. You'll be surprised what pops into your mind and comes up in your body.

Ask and Playfully Procrastinate

Similar to the walk, ask yourself, What do I want, and then do something that feels like play. Toss a ball with your kid, play solitaire, bake your favorite chocolate chip cookies. Your want will pop into your head, and you'll feel it in your gut.

Ask and Flip a Coin

If you're unsure about 2 distinct choices, get a coin to flip. You're not relinquishing the choice to the coin—you're using the coin to gather insight.

1. Assign 1 option or scenario heads and the other tails.
2. Flip the coin.
3. Observe your response.
   Your emotions will show you how you feel really fast. If you're disappointed by the result of the toss, you probably want the other option more.

Wanting is essential to clarity and joy. It's the spark that transforms *"we have to"* into *"what if we could?"*

Other Tools

These are helpful resources to have in your back pocket for difficult times.

HAALT

There's a reason you can buy a pillow embroidered with "I'm sorry for what I said when I was hungry," and the word "hangry" is common vocabulary. We logically know hunger makes it harder for us emotionally and mentally. So why would you make a decision in this state?

For years, rehab and addiction groups have used the HALT method to help people in recovery recognize triggers, make healthy decisions, and prevent relapse. I prefer the expanded HAALT: Hungry, Angry, Afraid, Lonely, Tired.

Hungry:	Angry:
This means literal belly-growling hunger and low blood sugar but also thirst and dehydration. Did you skip a meal? Have you had any water? Press pause on any decision until you've had a protein bar and water (not coffee!).	Anger about anything will block other Centers of Intelligence and other emotions you need to understand. Use Name-Rate-Find to process and lower the intensity. Don't make decisions when you're in the red zone of anger.
Afraid:	Lonely:
Fear also looks like anxiety and stress. When you feel fear, your brain says, "SURVIVE!" and moves into fight, flight, freeze, and fawn. You don't have all your brain working for you, so pause the decision. Emily P. Freeman has a great question that works well here: Am I being led by love or pushed by fear?	When you are isolated and feel like it's all on you, it's more than missing some outside perspectives. Your brain interprets loneliness as physical pain, which is why loneliness impairs your cognitive function. You have a hard time keeping relevant data in the forefront of your thoughts. When your working memory is low, you're making decisions without the needed facts and context. It also makes you tired because you carry more than you're designed to. Do I need a peer, a mentor, a coach, or a friend?

You can't outhustle your humanity. HAALT will keep you out of foolish decision-making.

Me, You, Now, or Later?

When the *do do do doda do do doo* of the *Jeopardy* theme song plays, you know you've got to make a decision by the last *doomda do do doo doo doo*. The time limit presses on you, making all things seem THE MOST IMPORTANT and RIGHT NOW. And if you face everything like a *Jeopardy* Final with a fortune on the line, you're not going to make great decisions.

Made famous as the Eisenhower Matrix, you can visually sort based on level of importance and urgency to remove the outside pressures of RIGHT NOW.

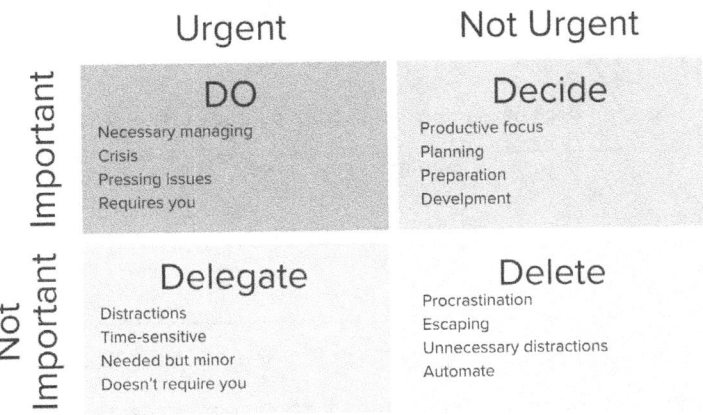

Jo Saxton, fellow author, speaker, and leadership expert, and I were talking on the *Joyosity* Podcast about our culture's tyranny of the urgent. She said, "The urgency that you're presenting has far more to do with your urgent need for me to react than my need to hear it right now."

The deeper power in this matrix comes when you realize you get to decide the urgency. Our culture wants everything yesterday, and you internalize that sense of urgency more often than you think. Come back to the matrix with your agency to assess true urgency.

Decision Insight Decoder

In *Joyosity*, the Decision Insight Decoder is the framework to help you use a wise process. Get all the pieces out of your head rather than endlessly ponder *What should I do?* You will reduce choices, find the right information, gather the right counsel, and maybe get a snack. Focus on the process, your choices, and your action steps—not the outcomes.

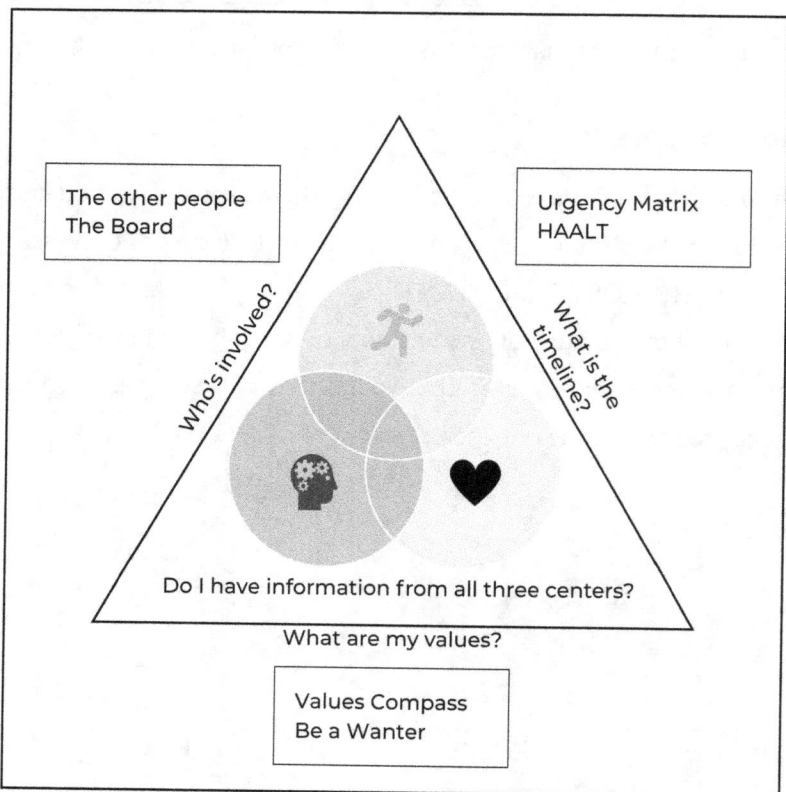

Remember there is no best decision. You always have choices and agency, but you will have more joy when you use your agency to make transparent decisions with a wise process.

You
can't
outsource
your
joy.

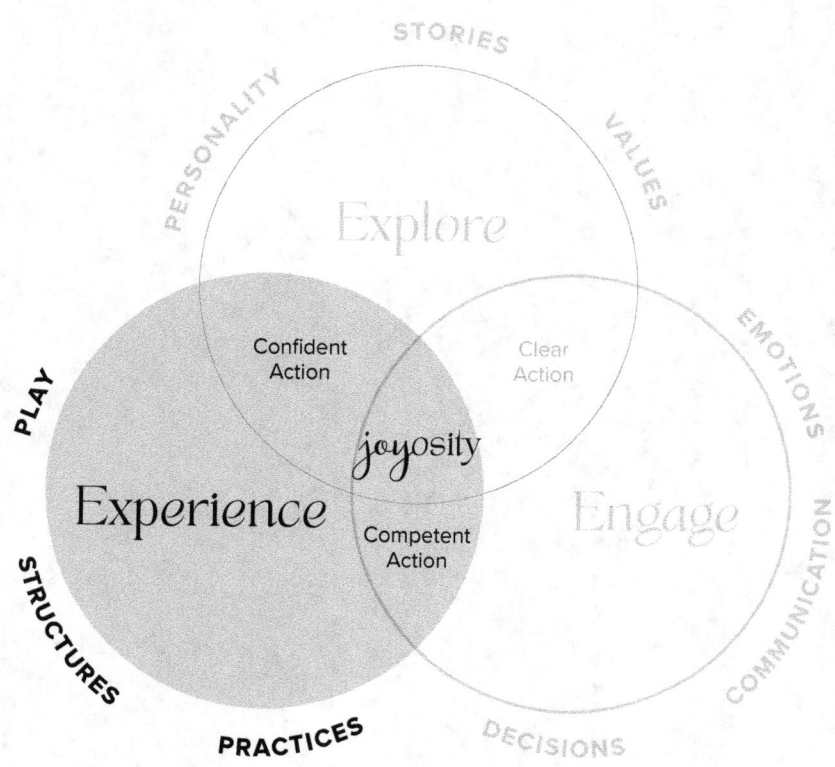

Part Three

Experience

Practice Makes Permanent

Plays that stay in the coach's file do nothing for the players. It's time to make this show up in your everyday, walking-around life.

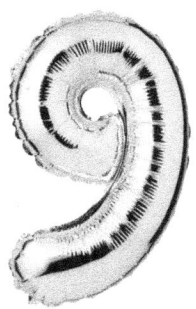

Regroup and Refuel

Practices move you into integration, one tiny choice at a time. In *Joyosity* chapters 10 and 11, you learned the purpose of practices and a few to start with.

"A practice is the embodiment of an approach to a concept."

—Rick Rubin

"A practice is anything you undertake with intention and breath."

— Peter O'Hanrahan

Practices are tiny actions that apply a healthy idea inside a moment of your life.

Joyosity discussed practices that close the stress cycle, give you space, create safety, and support your wholeheartedness. This chapter provides additional practices to bring you more joy overall.

Close the Cycle

As a brief review, the stress cycle is how your body responds to perceived threats or stressors: Your body moves through threat, response, release, and balance. Stress is psychological and neurological. You can't think your way out of stress. You must practice your way through. There are 7 ways to close the cycle: intense physical activity, breathwork, connecting with others, laughter, crying, affection, and creative work. We're going deeper with 3.

Ctrl + Alt + Breathe

Most of us are shallow breathers, even when we're not stressed. (Do you remember "screen apnea"? You stop breathing checking your email and scrolling screens.) Although breathing is an involuntary process, it's also your best intentional anytime, anywhere practice. Use one of these based on what you need. In the online resources, you'll find videos for each.

Whoosh and Go

If you hold your breath, need a quick reset, or a little help to shake off built-up tension, try this practice. Take a fast, but big, inhale, expanding both your chest and belly. Then audibly sigh and let all the air out with a "whoosh."

Four-Corner Calm

A general way to bring balance back to your nervous system is box breathing. Put one hand on your chest and the other on your belt (if you want to do this in the middle of a meeting, don't worry about your hands). Inhale evenly into your belt to the count of 4. Hold for 4. Exhale evenly for 4. Hold for 4. Repeat at least twice or until you feel a bit of good heaviness in your body. Two times is about 30 seconds; 4, about a minute.

Below the Buzz

If you're worked up and need to calm your energy before you lose your ish, grab this breath practice. Imagine your breath starts in your upper belly, and as you exhale it goes down. Your upper body stays still as you let the breath pull you underneath that buzzy energy and restore calm to your nervous system.

Pro tip: Trailblazers (Enneagram Three, Seven, and Eight) practice this type of breathing. You're typically comfortable with the higher energy of inhaling. You need to practice relaxing.

Open Chest Charge

If you're feeling low energy or need to gird your loins against Miranda Priestly, use this breath. Take a few large breaths between your collarbones and solar plexus. For this breath your shoulders and neck do not get to play, just your chest. Imagine you have a hot air balloon on the inside of your chest that is expanding up and out. Steady and managed, not erratic and fast. You want your energy up but not feeling like the balloon moved up into your head. If you get that light-headed feeling, take a break.

Pro tip: Professors (Enneagram Four, Five, and Nine) practice this type of breathing. Your lower energy level is connected to your comfort with exhaling. You need to practice expanding.

The Loooooong Exhale

If a few deep breaths don't restore your calm, try this one. The exhale of the anti-anxiety breath hangs out longer than the inhale took to come in. Imagine you've got a balloon in the center of your chest (your solar plexus) and you're filling that balloon. At the same time, you're also stretching the rubber band of your diaphragm. Breathe in for 4-6 counts and hold for 4-6. For the exhale, purse your lips like you're going to do a raspberry (or like you're going to make a squeaky sound with a balloon). Now slowly let the exhale push against your lips for 20-30 counts. While you're exhaling, let that balloon deflate as you relax your chest and the rubber band of your diaphragm loosen.

Go Where It Goes

For mindfulness and connection to yourself, use this receptive breath. You simply follow the breath with your attention. It's almost like the movie *Inner Space*; you're following your little spaceship inside yourself. Don't push to inhale or exhale any certain way, simply follow your breath. This breath is particularly effective if you're having trouble identifying your feelings or deciding what you want.

Pro tip: Connectors (Enneagram One, Two, and Six) practice this type of breathing. You mirror the breath of others, so you restrict both your inhale and exhale which depletes your energy. Practice attending to your own breath.

Social Connection

When you have something to celebrate or mourn, you want people to share it with. And when your nervous system kicks into high gear, even casual social interaction connects you with others and tells your body you're safe to calm down.

Got 8 Minutes?

To combat loneliness and close the stress cycle, hop on the phone with a friend. Walk with your neighbor. Get a coffee with that work buddy. Effective connection doesn't take long. Simon Sinek and Maria Shriver talk about being 8-minute friends on his *A Bit of Optimism Podcast* by texting each other "Got 8 minutes?" when they need to talk. Because 8-12 minutes is usually enough time to feel the effects of social connection.

List 2-3 friends who can be your 8-minute people. Send them a text or message and set up the request.

"Hey, I'm working on some stress management and joy-bringing practices. Do you have a few minutes to hop on the phone?"

Name	Sent message

Once you've established the 8-minute concept, you can just text: "Got 8 minutes?"

Get Micromoments

The social glue that lowers stress includes talking to strangers. Bestselling author and communication expert Vanessa Van Edwards calls them micromoments. She argues (and I agree) that "Airpods are killing friendship" because you retreat into your own world and miss the micromoments that communicate to your body *You're not alone.* Those tiny interactions in the hallway or the grocery aisle act as mortar to your community and career bricks. They absorb stress and help you close the stress cycle.

Social psychologists found consistent practice talking to strangers creates more optimism after just 1 week.

Practice Experiment: ⏱ 10 minutes 2x

Pick a day to experiment with one of these activities (or choose your own micromoment activity).

Say hi to 10 strangers (the store, the office, the street)	Ask "What's your day been like?" to make small talk (the elevator, in line at the store)	Spend a day without using headphones when you're in public
My idea:		

How do you feel about this? What do you think will happen?
How intense is your discomfort about this? 1   2   3   4   5   6   7   8   9   10

After your experiment, come back here.

How do you feel about the experience? What happened? What did you learn?
Compared to how you felt before, how intense is your discomfort now? 1   2   3   4   5   6   7   8   9   10

Creative Activities

Creativity is a proof of your humanity. Profit and productivity often exploit it instead of celebrating it. Returning to your creative, just-for-fun practices restores balance, connects you to your soul, and signals to your body, "You can complete the stress cycle, now."

Creative activities are not about the product. They are about the process of connecting to your humanity.

Quick Plays

Start with what you already like. These are easy supplies and activities to have at the ready when you notice your threat response kick in.

playdough	puzzles	gardening	watercolors	crafts
story prompt, journal	singing, instruments	sketching and drawing	cooking, baking	crayons, colored pencils, markers
sewing	yarn work	origami	woodworking	LEGO

The Long Game

Develop a hobby with your creative outlet. This means cultivating a creative practice over time that you participate in regularly.

Membership to a pottery studio, a writing group, a community choir, a cooking course...just follow the fun. Rick Rubin writes in *The Creative Act: A Way of Being*, "Excitement tends to be the best barometer for selecting which seeds to focus on."

> Having a regular practice of a creative outlet creates a greater sense of well-being and flourishing as well as a regulated nervous system.

> **Play It Out:**
> Choose 1 creative activity that feels fun and easy.
>
> Activity: _____
>
> Put it into a weekly block on your calendar for the next 4 weeks.

Space

From *Joyosity*, you'll know you need to create space to literally and figuratively breath. That means in the rushing, loud, and overly full world you need stillness, solitude, and silence.

Start small with 1 minute a day for 1 week with 1 practice. Record what you notice over the course of a week. Then extend your time in the stillness, solitude, or silence.

Day 1	Day 2	Day 3	Day 4	Day 5	Day 6	Day 7

Safety

You need to create an environment of safety, so, as Rubin writes, "you're free to express what you're afraid to express."

Watch the TRAIN ⏱ 3-?? minutes

If you don't have brain space because of intrusive thoughts, this is a practice for you.

You can't control the thoughts that come into your head. But you can train yourself to manage thoughts and choose what to do with them.

T—Tune In Get comfortable and close your eyes. Imagine you are at a train station, sitting on a comfortable bench on a beautiful day facing the tracks.

R—Recognize Observe your thoughts and imagine them as train cars sliding past you on the tracks and off around the bend.

A—Acknowledge When a new thought comes, place it on a train car.

I—Imagine You don't have to engage with the thought. Imagine it riding away.

N—Notice If the train yard gets busy, breathe and reimagine your lovely bench with you as the observer. Simply begin again.

You practice this as long as you need until you feel regulated and safe.

Morning Pages ⏱ 15 minutes

If your mind races the moment you open your eyes or as you lay your head on the pillow, this is a great practice for you. I adapted this Morning Pages activity from Julia Cameron's classic book, *The Artist's Way*.

1. Get blank paper and a pen or pencil. I recommend a spiral notebook or loose-leaf paper in a binder.

2. Write the date and start writing, stream of consciousness, until you fill 3 pages. Imagine your mind as tangled knots of yarn coming out into smooth skeins onto the page. You can't do this wrong! There's no judgement about what you write. No one else reads these pages. Cameron writes, "...morning pages are often negative, frequently fragmented, often self-pitying, repetitive, styled or babyish, angry or bland—even silly sounding. Good!"

3. When you fill 3 pages, stop. Don't reread them—throw them away. I KNOW! The point is to empty your mind of the fuzz, not to keep it! (This is especially powerful for the Idealists of the Enneagram—Ones, Fours, and Sevens.) If you

write something you desperately want to keep—a great turn of phrase, the appointment you need to remember to make—write it down on a Post-it, and throw away the rest.

You're creating safety to say the truthiest truths of the moment.

15-Minute Worry ⏱ 15 minutes

Much like intentional worry for Enneagram Sixes from chapter 2, this 15-Minute worry releases the clutter.

1. Get paper and a pen.
2. Set a timer for 15 minutes.
3. Worry. Start writing all the things that are currently worrying you. Then worry about all the things those situations could create. Get. It. All. Out. Worry like you've never been allowed to worry. If you come up with solutions during the 15 minutes, great. Write them down.
4. When the timer goes off, pencils down. Breathe, and release it all.

You'll find it's really hard to focus on worry for the full 15 minutes. I know you may say, "Try me." I promise, focused, intentional worry is different from the unproductive scenario building that's happening while you're trying to work on something else.

Achievement Archive ⏱ 1-5 minutes

Because you're a human, you have an *intense* bias toward negativity. But, as with many things that helped you survive, negativity bias towards yourself tanks your performance, drains your confidence, and makes you feel unsafe to celebrate the joy you bring to the world.

High-performing teams share about **6 positives for every negative**. Low-performing teams—**3 negatives for every positive**.

My friend Dr. Karen Doll, psychologist and author of *Building Psychological Fitness*, taught me about having your own "Personal Book of Awesome." It's not a gratitude journal. It's a practice to counteract the natural tendency to see mostly the negative by recording your wins.

Not only is this great for performance reviews, but it also builds evidence for your self-efficacy work from chapter 3. You're building safety for joy in your life because celebrating rewires your brain to honestly see your accomplishments, contributions, and your progress over time.

1. Get a dedicated notebook, journal, file on your computer, or place in your planner.
2. Write the date and jot down the win(s).

    The compliment your colleague gave you, praise from a client, a positive moment with a coworker you find challenging, you met your water goal for the day. Nothing is too small or big.

No need for essays—just enough for future you to remember the moment and how it felt. I do this weekly with my Joyosity Leadership Lab clients, and I'm working on making it daily for myself.

Here are a few examples from flipping through my planner on my desk:

- Asked for my own connecting flight to Memphis instead of literally running to catch the next flight that the airline rebooked me on. I can ask for what I need. I don't have to just accept what's given.
- Client feedback after a keynote: "Jenn's professionalism and presence are unmatched. Her talk was deeply inspiring and engaging and something everyone should care about."
- Got to hold a real copy of my first book!
- I gave Carrie a gift that she loved and totally surprised her.
- I didn't lose my temper when my son lost his ever-loving mind.

You can extend this practice in a number of ways, but simply start regularly recording your wins.

Support

As a culture, we push past any and all healthy support systems that are hardwired into your humanity. *Sleep is lazy. You don't need anyone else. Food is just fuel.* Lies! All lies!

On the flip side, we confuse normal discomfort or difficulty with the extreme problem of burnout. And burnout's become one of those words we toss around like "love." I love confetti. I love my husband. I'm burned out on Instagram. That pitcher burned out his arm.

No wonder it's hard to tell what burnout really means. We're so desensitized to living on fire, we don't even notice burnout.

Burnout Check-in

The World Health Organization classifies burnout as a disease characterized by 3 dimensions:

- "I wake up exhausted."
  Feelings of energy depletion or exhaustion.

- "I don't even have it in me to care."
  Increased mental distance from life's activities, feelings of negativity, or cynicism about life.

- "I can't seem to focus or finish anything."
  Reduced professional and personal productivity and fruitfulness.

> **Burnout** is a syndrome from chronic stress that has not been successfully managed—individually, organizationally, and systemically.

There are multiple technical tools to measure burnout, but this is a simple burnout check-in so you can separate everyday fatigue from real burnout. Not as fun as a Buzzfeed quiz, but way more useful.

Burnout Barometer ⏱ 5-15 minutes

Ruthless self-honesty and radical self-compassion will give you clarity. Think of this as an informal snapshot of a moment in time.

Physical Symptom Check: Mark all that you've experienced over the last month.	
☐ Digestive problems	☐ Unexplained aches and pains
☐ Chronic fatigue	☐ High blood pressure
☐ Sleep issues	☐ Shortness of breath/racing heart
☐ Physical illness	☐ Difficulty focusing on tasks
☐ Appetite changes	☐ Headaches
☐ Misuse of food, drugs, or alcohol	☐ Sensory overload
Total:	
4 or fewer: *Tolerable.* But keep an eye on it.	**5 or more:** *Concerning. It's time to address issues.*

Self-Examination: For each statement, rate how often you experience it, then total your points.					
Energy	**Not often**	**Once a month**	**Once a week**	**Most days**	**Every day**
I feel drained and weary—physically or emotionally at the end of my rope.	1	2	3	4	5
It's hard to be understanding or empathetic with people. They don't get me either.	1	2	3	4	5
Engagement					
I wonder if what I do matters at all.	1	2	3	4	5
I am irritated by or hypercritical of my colleagues.	1	2	3	4	5
Pressure					
The pressure to succeed to high standards feels uncomfortable.	1	2	3	4	5
I have more work than I can actually do, let alone do well.	1	2	3	4	5
Productivity					
It's challenging to focus or concentrate.	1	2	3	4	5
The structures or culture in my work prevent me from getting work done.	1	2	3	4	5
Harmony					
I find it difficult to unwind or turn off.	1	2	3	4	5
My work intrudes on or interferes with the rest of my life.	1	2	3	4	5
Total:					

15 or lower: *Tolerable—unless you have more than one 5.*	**16-25:** *Take care. This looks like low-level burnout.*
26-35: *You are in moderate burnout and at risk for deteriorating further.*	**36 or higher:** *You're in intense burnout. Address this urgently.*

If you're in the **tolerable** range, keep practicing what you've learned in *Joyosity*. You'll build resilience and prevent burnout from intensifying.

If you're in **low-level**, **moderate**, or **intense burnout**, please don't go it alone. It's time to get help. If you could fix it by yourself, you already would have. The longer burnout goes unaddressed, the longer recovery takes.

Let you your people in—friends, family, your Personal Board, your doctor, or HR. Find a professional coach or therapist to help you heal.

Tiny actions are tremendous—but tricky to start and sustain. An outside voice helps you spot what's hiding in plain sight, hold you accountable, and remind you of what is practical in your real life. I offer 15-minute Spark Calls and 30-minute Breakthrough sessions as well as other coaching programs to help you develop the practices that sustain your joy.

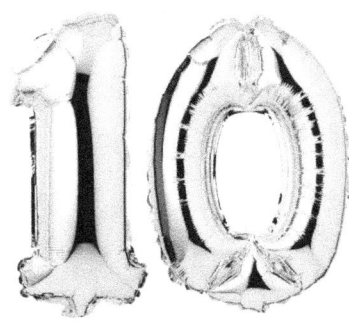

Build Training Habits

Do you want to keep doing the work you love and protect your joy when things are what they are? Then you need steady structures that put practices into automatic, repeatable patterns. You need to establish structures unique to your values and personality, flexible enough to shift with new seasons, and strong enough to sustain you when the sea of life is rough. Steady structures have 3 layers: systems to free you, rhythms to steady you, and rituals to ground you.

Systems: Anything repeatable and interconnected that enables your favorite self to do your best work. Basically, a system is *when I do xyz, I do it this way*.

Rhythms: A sequence of actions or pauses that you repeat regularly.

Rituals: A sequence of activities that mark the transition from one activity, posture, or experience to another.

A system can be delegated, outsourced, or automated. Rhythms and rituals are embodied. They require you to show up for yourself.

This section helps you build the structures for how your life actually works. You'll find reflection prompts and planning space to experiment with structures to build an experience of joy.

Most people make progress by taking this section in small parts, or by setting aside a focused block of time to step back and look at the big picture of what you need. You can work through this section on your own—or, if you'd like guidance and accountability, schedule a **Design Day,** and we'll design it together.

Why and a White Board

The activities are *integrated*, so before you decide if you're going to put your gift list in flimlfip.com or the zipidee doodah app, you have to know why you need the system and what you want it to do. The same idea goes for rhythms and rituals. Once you've made choices for each type of structure, you'll put them all together.

Building Systems

A system is not a tech tool. You build your system based on need, then choose the best tool that works for you.

Harvard Business Review studied CEOs and found that reliable systems saved them from redoing work and overriding decisions.

Questions you must answer first:

- What decisions/activities do I repeat?
- What questions come up all the time?
- How do I want to engage with people?
- Where do my appointments and time commitments live?
- How do I track to-dos, tasks, deliverables?
- What needs to be visible to more people? How do I share information?
- Where do I get stuck?
- Who or what is the bottleneck?
- What can be decision-treed? If this happens, then x. If that happens, then y.
- What can be automated?

Choose 1 system to test. Go to a whiteboard or grab some Post-its. When you're designing, you need to move individual stages around.

When I coach clients through this process, we stand and move around to visualize the process. Map the steps and adjust until you feel ready to test it.

Rhythm by Design

Again, we're starting with questions at the white board, Post-its, or big paper calendars. Questions:

- What practices do you want to make habits and downbeats in your life? Daily, weekly, monthly, annually?
- What tasks, practices, or activities do you want to make time for? Go back to your Joyosity Explorer Map and which practices bring you space, safety, and support.
- What are your regular responsibilities? What are the typical commitments that you need to fulfill?
- Can you negotiate or delegate any of your responsibilities, commitments, or obligations?

Rhythm Styles

Next, you need to choose if you are a Manager, a Maker, or a Musician. Remember, these are personas not actual career titles!

Managers: See work through calendar blocks. Their days move in 30- or 60-minute segments. Managers think by the clock, moving from task to task, activity to activity.

Makers: Think in projects, not hours. Need long, uninterrupted stretches to create or think or do deep work. Work best in 3- to 4-hour segments of time or sometimes day segments: morning, afternoon, evening.

Musicians: Work in days. They batch similar work for the day, giving each day its own focus. Musicians work best with harmony among creation, preparation, and rest.

Choosing your rhythm style.

1. If you were starting the world of work from scratch, how would you structure your time for the most ease and productivity?
   a. I like short blocks of time.
   b. I prefer a couple of hours without interruption.
   c. I do best when my work has a focus or theme for long periods of time—a day or even a week.

2. How do interruptions impact your work?
   a. I can switch from task to task and stay on track.
   b. One meeting in the middle of the morning wrecks my focus.
   c. I need one or the other. I can have a planned day of multiple things, but I need another full day for creation or rest.

3. What makes a great day for you?
   a. Checking things off my prioritized list and managing my meeting times.
   b. Making progress on a project because I had time to think.
   c. Feeling in deep flow because I could put all my energy to 1 area of focus.

4. When do you feel the most recharged or effortlessly productive?
   a. Moving through the calendar and tasks for the day on time.
   b. After completing a project or making a breakthrough in solving a problem.
   b. After a long stretch of time doing the same type of work or for the same project.

Mostly As: Manager

Mostly Bs: Maker

Mostly Cs: Musician

Which are you choosing? _____

Rituals: Walking through doors

Rituals help you mentally, emotionally, and physically move smoothly through phases of your day and your life. They are tiny doorways that sustain your joy as you move through them.

Questions for rituals are a little more contemplative:

- What are your transitions during your day?
- Where do you feel the most pinched during the day?
- How do you want to feel at the end of the day?
- What are the different roles you play during the day?
- How much time and how do you need to process feelings and events?
- What types of energy shifts do you need?
- What times of the year are hardest for you?
- What practices do you need to transition well?

Create your rituals for these situations. Here's a quick review of the 4 rituals from chapter 12 in *Joyosity* plus a ritual for other transitions.

Work Shutdown Ritual

1. Review and adjust your task list from the day.
2. Record a win.
3. Review your schedule for tomorrow.
4. Set your Top Three for the next day.
5. Gather the junk. Close the clutter.
6. Close the door.

Evening Ritual

1. Put your house and phone to bed.
2. Pick your clothes and pack your bags.
3. Care for your body, heart, and mind.

Morning Ritual

1. Care for your body, heart, and mind.
2. Open the house.
3. Greet your people.

Work Startup Ritual

1. Set the stage.
2. Big loud purpose.
3. Review your top tasks and appointments.

Goodbye Hello
This ritual helps you mark an ending and open space for what's next. It could be closing out your week before starting a new one—I call this my Sunday Summit. Marking the end of a school year, saying goodbye to summer and welcoming autumn, or leaving a role and moving to a new one are all Goodbye Hello opportunities.

Other Rituals
Anytime you need to transition, you can ground yourself with a simple ritual. Rituals are great for moments like these: pre- and post-talk or presentations, opening and closing meetings, celebrations and milestones, returning from vacation or travel, beginning or ending creative work, shifting from solo work to interactive times.

Design As If

It's time to design your experience—your Designed Week.* Imagine you have the final say over every bit of your time. (Well, you do, but we don't live like that.) Design your week from that idea, as if you always had full control.

1. Choose your Designed Week Grid based on your Rhythm Style from the Fillable Frameworks.
2. Add in your rituals based on when they happen in the rhythm of your days and week. Colored pencils work great for this activity.
3. Add any responsibilities—weekly visit with your grandma, pickleball league, carpool, standing meetings—that are pretty much on repeat.
4. Add time for any practices you want to make time for.
5. Add blocks for processing email, creative time, theme days, etc.
6. Choose what systems you'll use to support your Designed Week.

Pro Tip: You're building a framework for flexibility that builds on who you are. If you've never been a 5am person, don't build a 5am morning ritual. Start with less and add more as you go.

Once you get the flow of living with your Designed Week, you can add goals, quarterly rocks, and annual focus.

*I've adapted this process from Michael Hyatt, Paul Graham, Dan Sullivan, and Dr. Benjamin Hardy.

Evolve Your Structure

My dad loves sandwiches, pasta, and biscuits. About 10 years ago, doctors diagnosed my carb-loving dad with celiac disease. After decades, he needed to change his structures.

Your structures are not Stonehenge. They are strong but flexible.

You should revisit and redesign:

- Quarterly
- When circumstances change
- When it's not working or producing joy

Start again with the questions and redesign.

The right systems, rhythms, and rituals bring ease, clarity, and joy. If you're ready to create steady structures that work with your life, not against it, let's design them together in a **Design Day.**

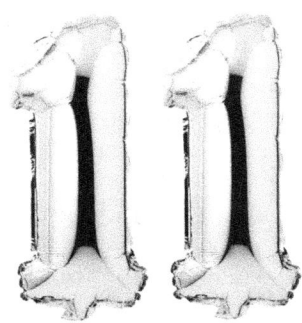

Put Play to Work

Play is a state of being, not an activity.

The state of play includes characteristics or properties including:

- Apparently purposeless
- Voluntary
- Attractive or novel
- Free from a sense of time
- Unselfconscious, fully present
- Has improv potential
- Continuation desire
- Risky

When you don't play: Absenteeism rises, creativity and collaboration drop significantly. You lack resilience and flexibility to face new challenges and problems, often feeling helpless. The other direction is overwork and a culture of sacrificing for the job. And you may even become the office bully.

Play has huge payoffs: Collaboration, connection, creativity, productivity, and innovation all increase. Your communication and relationships are stronger, and you establish clear norms that create a sticky culture where people perform better and stay longer. Through the experience of play, you increase your tolerance for discomfort and develop a radical acceptance of reality. Finally, play can change the mood in a moment and, over time, will quite literally keep you sane.

Play is how you develop mastery, expertise, and resilience. All the data and research are available in *Joyosity*. Let's jump into discovering how honing your natural play style will lead to mastery and how to use play to solve problems.

Play Styles

Everyone plays, but not everyone plays the same way. Some not only appeal to you, they feel like the way you're stitched together. This is what Dr. Stuart Brown identified as "play styles." In his research, he found 8 personas that exemplified the style of play that came most naturally to people. I've built on his work and blended it with my observations and experiences with clients to bring these 8 characters to life for you:

1. The Collector
2. The Competitor
3. The Creator
4. The Director
5. The Explorer
6. The Kinesthete
7. The Jester
8. The Storyteller

Most people have 1 dominant style with 2 supporting styles. Your special trio—that lead singer and the bandmates—forms how you naturally lean into play. It directs you to activities at work that feel effortless, energizing, and exciting.

Finding your Play Trio

Before we audition some personas, we need to get into the wayback machine.

What were your favorite toys or activities in elementary school?

What activities were the most boring in middle school? (Not because you were trying to play it cool.)

Ok, now let's go back to the future.

Imagine it's 10 years from now. You only have to do 5 things you truly love—what makes the list?

Ten years from now, what's something that—if you never did it again—it'd still be too soon?

Ok, we're back to right now

Revisit your Joy-Giving list from the Joyosity Explorer Map. What feels like play to you on that list?

In the past 3 months, what compliments have surprised you because the work or activity felt easy—or even fun?

Auditioning the Players

You're meeting a few potentials, seeing who feels familiar, fun, and the right fit. Much like discovering your Enneagram type and uncovering your core values, go with your gut and the feels. Don't get too analytical here. You can't do this wrong. As you read, put a little star by the ones that feel like you and an X next to the ones that are a hard pass.

The Collector

Gathering is a joy for you. You may be the garage sale specialist or the one who scratches off all the baseball parks you've been to. The curation of a theme thrills you. And the work of finding it and recording it is as meaningful as having it.

You may be a sommelier, sportscaster, archivist, librarian, CPA, historian, gardener, data analyst, creator, curator, records manager, editor, designer, scientist, or the person who loves collecting as a way to experience the world.

Through your craft you bring details and history to a professional level, supporting everyone in knowing the details and where to find them.

Your Edge: Gathering, organizing, and curating information or experiences.

Power Plays: Tracking details, creating systems, structuring workflows, project management, research.

In the Wild: You've got a detailed spreadsheet of every Indian restaurant you've ever been to.

The Competitor

Competition? You're all in, and you're winning it. Pursuing victory is the best part of the game, and really all of life. Watching a competition or competing yourself, you get energy from the strategy, focus, and effort winning requires.

You may be an athlete, coach, finance professional, politician, entrepreneur, marketer, strategist, litigator, investment banker, sales professional, or the one on the team who's always ready to create a game and win. Through your craft, you find strategies and creative methods to achieve the goal.

Your Edge: Energized by challenges, clear goals, and measurable success.

Power Plays: Setting benchmarks, tracking progress, encouraging friendly competition to motivate the team (and yourself), recognizing and awarding achievements, creating gamification.

In the Wild: Beating the GPS-time is your extreme sport (and you win every time).

The Creator

You see what others cannot. You seem to make beauty out of thin air. You transform abstract ideas into something others can experience. You may paint, craft, bake, sculpt, garden, write, design, build, code, decorate, or woodwork—you use your imagination and your hands to bring things to life.

You could be an artist, designer, chef, baker, experience designer, museum curator, interior designer, app coder, innovator, or entrepreneur. You use your craft to bring beauty and function into the world.

Your Edge: Bringing ideas to life through imagination and hands-on creativity.

Power Plays: Innovative problem-solving, complex systems thinking, design, and processes improvement.

In the Wild: You have a supply closet, shed, and an overflow bin for "future projects."

The Director

You're happy in charge and making things happen feels like child's play to you. You're a natural leader found organizing, arranging, throwing parties, creating a system, managing large groups to a goal...basically, you turn chaos into order with ease and a smile.

You may be a project manager, a cross-functional team leader, a systems specialist, an operations director, a volunteer organizer, an event planner, a producer, a director, a coach, an administrator, a teacher, or a restaurant manager. Through your craft, you get ideas and people into action.

Your Edge: Organizing, planning, and making things happen.

Power Plays: Bring ideas into being by managing people, leading the leader, supervising projects, and coordinating logistics.

In the Wild: Someone thought you worked at Costco because you were telling the team members how to set up the end cap.

The Explorer

With curiosity as your North Star, you love exploring life. There is always something new to learn or create or see. From traveling to experiencing a new song, what's on the horizon always seems like fun. You play when researching or experimenting or looking for the other perspectives.

You may be a scientist, inventor, performer, speaker, creator, entrepreneur, innovator, traveler, tour guide, farmer, astronaut, or simply the one who's always ready to try something new as a leader. Through your craft, you help bring the groundbreaking new ideas to life and bring people along with you in the inevitable sea of changes.

Your Edge: Discovering new ideas, experiences, and perspectives.

Power Plays: Curiosity, problem-solving, innovation, and inspiring teams to think outside the box, experimentation and beta-testing, managing change, researching new trends, or early adoption.

In the Wild: While booking flights, you end up down the Reddit rabbit hole of how street food fuels the economy of Fukuoka, Japan.

The Jester

Jokes are like breathing to you. You may have been the class clown or the court jester. You play with the absurdity of life with witty comments, funny stories, or even pranks on the people you spend time with.

You may be a performer, communicator, humorist, writer, content creator, journalist, copywriter, or trainer. Through your craft, you help people find the lighter side of the difficulty of being human.

Your Edge: Bringing energy, humor, and levity to every situation.

Power Plays: Easing tension, driving engagement, encouragement when the situation looks bleak, bringing a reality check in intensity, shifting the mood, modeling the freedom to fail.

In the Wild: Forget New Year's Eve. April Fool's Day is your holiday.

The Kinesthete

Movement flows from you. The pure joy and freedom of moving your body is far more fun than winning the game. You come alive in movement and connecting to your body, possibly even pushing it to the extremes. You find wisdom when you move your body.

You may be an athlete, dancer, yogi, massage therapist, circus artist, choreographer, athletic trainer, firefighter, or occupational therapist. Through your craft, you use your body to improve the lives of others.

Your Edge: Using movement and physical activity for learning, connection, and problem-solving.

Power Plays: Stand-up meetings, walking brainstorms, hands-on projects, interactive experiences.

In the Wild: Sometimes you miss dance class because you've got a pickleball game.

The Storyteller

Playing always means a story for you! You don't simply take stories in; you experience them. The emotions, the characters, the atmosphere... you create the world in your imagination. In your everyday life, you think about your life as a collection of microstories, weaving facts with experience.

Life is a stage, and you are the one telling the story. You may be a communicator, content creator, writer, speaker, playwright, teacher, or screenwriter. Your style of play as a craft takes the narrative and makes it real to others.

Your Edge: Connecting ideas and people through compelling narratives.

Power Plays: Communicating vision, selling, engaging audiences, making information memorable, raising money, contextualizing data.

In the Wild: When you're walking the dog, you see two neighbors chatting over the fence, and you think, "This is a great story about community and everyday interactions that is perfect for that client presentation."

The Callbacks

Go back through your stars and pick your top 3 that feel the most like you.

- _____
- _____
- _____

From this list, which is the lead and who are the backup singers? If you're not sure, review your answers from the questions at the start of this section.

Lead Persona: _____

Back-up Personas: _____ _____

When you find your play persona and focus on developing it, you don't only change how work feels (because yes, please, let it feel like play), but you also change how work works. You the find unique success, that Jade Simmons calls your "differentiator."

Play to Solve

Especially if you're not practiced at playing, you need a little warm up before jumping into play at work. Typically you need to bring the energy up and loosen up a bit. Both of these activities can be done alone or with others.

Play Warmups

Skips and Sass

Start saying this phrase "skips and sass" over and over. Exaggerate the sounds, beat box them, say them faster and faster, add accents, just keep repeating until it all blends together and it seems ridiculous, or you're giggling. Typically this is less than 2 minutes. This feels like pure silliness (which is fine!), but it also physically prepares your body to engage and activates those play circuits.

Crazy Counts

Alone or with others in a circle, count down from 6 while shaking your right hand, then counting down from 6 with your left hand, then right leg, then left leg. Start again with the right hand and count down from 5. Repeat the pattern until you get to 1-1-1-1. As you get comfortable with playing, have folks choose a funny voice or accent for each number like Six: French Queen, Five: Mountain Man, Four: New Yorker, Three: Helium, Two: Whisper, One: Shout. If you want to lengthen the exercise, count down from a higher number.

Play to Solve

What if?

Futurists don't predict the future, but they do help people prepare for possibilities by harnessing foresight. This activity works as a playful conversational approach that brings some of the power of futurists into your meetings.

This activity works solo or in a group. In What If? you are not bound by any old ways, rules, or even laws of physics. Literally let anything be possible. (I do suggest you stay within your values, but you can play around with it.)

1. Let's do a "What if?" Start with naming that you're playing, "Let's do a 'what if.'" The purpose is to create scenarios, possible, probable, even impossible.
2. Change one thing and create 3 stories or scenarios. What if we didn't send a weekly newsletter to our list?

    a. If we didn't send a weekly email, all of our clients would forget we exist. Our amazing company would slowly evaporate from the marketplace with zero brand presence.

   b. If we didn't send a weekly email, we could send a shorter email every day that our clients could use. And they would start calling us more because they're reading the email.

   c. If we didn't send a weekly email, we could send individual messages to hottest leads and create a white paper to pitch news organizations. Our pipeline shrinks at first but because we convert more of our hottest leads and serve them well, they keep referring us to other people. The white paper lives online so new leads who are looking for us find us when they're searching specifically.

(This example is a little more rooted in reality, but you can throw ridiculous things on the table to simply open up possibilities. We learn telepathy. We Joker-style hypnotize people with the extra time we have from not creating emails.)

3. Rate the story. Use a scale of 1 to 7 with 1 as the low end.
   a. How likely or possible is this story to you? 1 is the low end. (You'll be surprised how different people answer!).
   b. On the scale, how worried (low end) or excited (high end) are you about this story?
   c. How equipped do you feel to work through this story if it were true?

4. Now what? Based on the scenarios and ratings, what new ideas or possibilities do you have?

You can always do it again and change options. Often one time through, opens up the brain and new ideas come without continuing the play version of What If? There are multiple ways to do this. You can create it by timeline. What if... If we did x, in 2 months this, in 6 months this, in a year this.

FACTS

This activity works well after playing and warmup activities. It's technically not play, but it's an alternative problem-solving activity that creates flow and moves you to taking action.[*] If you want to toss a ball, fidget with an object, or walk while doing this, totally encouraged.

For this activity, you need a partner or groups of two. One person is the Factfinder, the other is the Facilitator.

Factfinder: You are the one actively solving the problem. You're the speaker.

Facilitator: You are the questioner and listener. You are a mostly silent partner.

Find and Face

Facilitator: "Where is the problem?"

Factfinder: Imagine the problem and locate the problem in the space around you. Is it by your hip? Is it out the side door? Is it a circle around you. There is no right or wrong answer. Allow your gut to tell you where it is. Tell the facilitator where it is. (Not the details of the problem.)

Facilitator: "What have you not faced about this yet?" [Then stay silent. Do not interrupt.]

Factfinder: Tell the facilitator what you've not faced about the problem. Name the things you've not said out loud. The part that's true you don't want to be true. Anything you've not faced about the problem. Just let everything come out.

Facilitator: [when the Factfinder stops] "Anything else?"

Factfinder: If there's more, share more.

Facilitator: Repeat "Anything else?" until the Factfinder says no.

Now you can move to the next step.

Accept

Facilitator: "What have you not accepted about this yet?"

Factfinder: Tell the facilitator what you've not accepted about the problem or situation. Again, this is whatever you've not accepted. Could be your true feelings, that you can't change this, could be that it's uncomfortable. Notice and name without judging.

Facilitator: [when the Factfinder stops] "Anything else?"

Factfinder: If there's more, share more.

Facilitator: Repeat "Anything else?" until the Factfinder says no.

---

[*] Adapted from Gillian Ferrabee.

Now you can move to the next step.

Choose and Commit

Facilitator: "What's your new story?"

Factfinder: Choose a new story (SNAP it up!) You may try out a couple new stories.

Facilitator: "What are you committing to?"

Factfinder: Name and commit to the new mindset. "I'm committing to..."

Facilitator: Repeat "Anything else?" until the Factfinder says no.

Now you can move to the next step.

Take Action

Facilitator: "What action do you want to take?"

Factfinder: Create an action step with a quantitative result and deadline. The action needs to be small enough to start within 3 days and finish within a month. Talk it out until it's concise and clear.

Facilitator: "What is your action, and when will you complete it?"

Factfinder: Repeat it in 1 sentence, "You will find 3 options for a new internal communication tool by November 4."

Salute

Facilitator: "What will you do to celebrate when you finish?

Factfinder: Choose a celebration or reward for finishing. It does not have to be expensive or elaborate. But choose a reward for yourself. I will go to a movie with friends. I will go to the driving range alone. I will go to the bookstore for an afternoon. I will buy the newest BÉIS bag. Pick a reward to salute your completion.

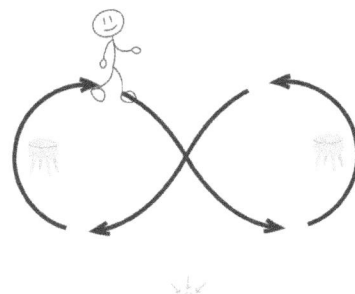

Variation: If you feel stuck, like the words aren't coming, try this physical reset: the infinity loop.

Set 2 chairs or objects about 6 to 8 feet apart. Find a point to focus on that is out in front of the center of the chairs. It can be the Facilitator or another point. Walk an infinity loop pattern in a smooth motion while always keeping your head and eyes on the focus point. You'll have to twist your midsection and neck to keep your eyes on the focus point while your body moves. Try to walk as smoothly as possible around the loop.

You may feel a little discomfort or an odd feeling at the intersection. That's normal. Keep going. Continue to look at the focus point and keep talking.

When I lead groups through these activities, play opens up better collaboration, new solutions, and new workflows. Because when you know your play persona and your mastery activities, you can use them on purpose and find a lighter way to lead. Because play powers productivity.

Are you audacious enough for joy?

Play it Forward

The players drilled *Pepper Shakers, Midnight Poutine, Upside-Down Taxi,* and unified as a team. Against seemingly insurmountable odds, they believed in shaking up the game. They ran the wildest play of all in the last minute of the game and tied up the score. With seconds left, an opponent broke away and scored 1 final goal—a 2-1 loss to the best team in the league.

In the locker room after the game, the coach told the truth: "This loss hurts. Even though you didn't win, you definitely succeeded."

Coach was right. **Winning at the cost of your joy is failure.**

And in the long run, joy outplayed the hustle. The team played from joy, got promoted, and built a better life on and off the field.

That's your work with this Playbook. You won't master every play on the first try—or maybe even the fifth. Some experiments will fall flat. Others will surprise you when an inch of change opens up a mile of success. Every time you try one of these plays, you're strengthening your joy muscles and creating a culture that multiplies joy for everyone around you.

Joyosity isn't one game. It's the ongoing practice of playing for joy, again and again.

- **Keep practicing.** Come back to these pages. Revisit your Joy Ratio. Rerun the plays that worked and tweak the ones that didn't. You build joy through repetition and a willingness to stay in the game—even when the scoreboard doesn't show the win yet.

- **Share what you're learning.** Talk about the plays that make a difference in your team meetings, one-on-ones, and that group text with your best friends (You know, the one with all the GIFs). The fastest way to make joy stick in your life is sharing it with others.

- **Find your Joyosity Team.** Invite your colleagues, friends, or whole teams to play with you. You'll find that joy grows faster when you have fellow teammates.

When you need a coach to run plays and cheer from the bench, I'm here. I'd love to help you succeed in leadership and build a life of real joy.

Joy doesn't guarantee the win every time.

Joy has dirt on its face and determination in its eye because joy finds what's possible and good without denying the difficulty and the pain.

Joy has laughter in its mouth because joy has the absolute audacity to believe the future belongs to those who pursue it.

Go take the field. Have the audacity to play it forward with joy.

Appendix A: Enneagram Type Descriptions

Body Group

Enneagram Eight: The Protective Challenger

Trusted Tactic	Protect
Fundamental Fear	Being vulnerable, powerless, weak, controlled, or manipulated
Driving Desire	To protect yourself and those closest to you
Persistent Pattern	Excess and intensity
Lasting Longing	You will not be betrayed
Anger goes outward | Trailblazer | Dynamite	

Strong and protective, Enneagram Eights don't show weakness, fearing someone may control or manipulate them if they do. Rather than risk being played like a puppet—or worse, betrayed—they snip the strings and take charge themselves. For an Eight, protecting themselves (and those they allow inside their castle keep) always takes first priority. Others can feel as if they take charge with the force of a tsunami. If there's a leadership vacuum, you can bet an Eight will stride forward to fill it and manage that scene. To the Eight, taking charge is the only way not to end up powerless (even though, sometimes, they'd like for someone they trust to do it for them.)

Eights, especially women, get a bad rap often as bitches or bullies. While their protective streak can drive them in that direction, they're often simply the only ones willing to take responsibility or state the hard truth. At times, they simply don't understand why others don't want that too. This persistent pattern to push hard in every direction creates an intensity that others don't always know what to do with. Because they value honesty and directness, you'll rarely have to guess how an Eight feels. They have the most amount of energy of all the types, and they trust their gut. They see the entire system and solve problems quickly—often before others have even processed the situation. If they trust someone else's authority, Eights can happily follow, even relishing the relief of not always having to be the strong one. But at the whiff of weakness or manipulation, Eights rush right back into the driver's seat.

Eights want belonging, but they'll settle for power.

At their best, Eights lower the bar for trusting others and use their strength to care for people in genuine, tender ways. Because really, Eights have a gooey center of compassion hidden by a rougher exterior. Ultimately, Eights remind us that real power doesn't come from dominating others. They show us how to create belonging by standing firm for what's right and shielding those who need protection. When they harness their fierce energy for good, Eights become unstoppable champions of justice and loyalty.

Enneagram Nine: The Harmonious Peacemaker

Trusted Tactic	Withdraw
Fundamental Fear	Loss of connection and belonging, conflict, being overlooked
Driving Desire	Internal and external harmony, stability, and peace
Persistent Pattern	Disengagement
Lasting Longing	Your presence matters
Ignores the anger | Professor | Silver Lining	

Easy-going and accommodating, Enneagram Nines desire both internal and external harmony—and they really want others to chill out too. If folks around them don't respond with a similar vibe, Nines will merge with what others want, just to keep the peace. They believe their deepest fear is conflict, but underneath, it's loss of connection. Nines believe if they assert their independence and autonomy, they'll lose connection and belonging. Instead of voicing their own ideas and feelings, they fall into patterns of indecision, procrastination, and disengagement. Broom in hand, sweeping difficulties right under the rug, often sounds like, "Whatever you think. I don't know. That's not really my job." Sometimes, it looks like daydreaming or escaping to numbing activities (Netflix and a cozy blanket, anyone?).

To manage the compulsion to maintain peace and an even-tempered image, Nines avoid disagreement. Preserving all that peace leaves them disconnected from their own wants, needs, and sense of worth, creating a deep lack of harmony within themselves. Ironically, Nines are the most stubborn of the Enneagram type structures. Because they want to maintain that easy-going image, they find subtle ways to resist rather than an outright no. One of their go-tos? Adjusting the pace. Push a Nine to hurry, and they will find a lower gear you didn't know existed. No conflict to see here, just a slowdown.

Nines want to be connected, but they'll settle for keeping the peace.

At their best, Nines build consensus with their ability to see all sides of an issue. They show up to the table ready to contribute thoughtfully and confidently while smoothly incorporating what others bring, cultivating belonging. In this space, Nines show us that real connection isn't keeping the peace; it's making peace by valuing everyone in the process, including themselves.

Enneagram One: The Reforming Perfectionist

Trusted Tactic	Perfect
Fundamental Fear	Being bad or wrong, unredeemable, misaligned, rude, or corrupt
Driving Desire	Goodness and rightness
Persistent Pattern	Resentment
Lasting Longing	You are good.
Anger goes inward	Connector	Cool Cucumber	

Principled and ever-improving, Enneagram Ones strive to make everything and everyone better—no detail too small, no spreadsheet too color-coded. Fueled by a deep desire to be good all the way through, Ones fear any hint of flaws or wrongdoing because they believe that negates their goodness. If they'll admit it, Ones fight the story that one mistake isn't a blip; it's a black mark that means they're bad. Enter the ever-present inner critic, barking orders like the middle school queen bee who dangles belonging and then changes the rules. "Yes, you finished that project, but you should have done more." This internal scorekeeper keeps them locked in perfection mode.

Others can feel as if Ones always need to be right, but it's really that they want to be in "rightness," aligned with the external rules (and whatever that tiny, yet loud critic is berating them about in the moment). So if you feel like Ones are hypercritical externally, that is only a fraction of the intensity of their internal criticism of themselves.

All that drive for precision simmers into frustration when the world refuses to meet their standards, leaving Ones feeling like they're the only adults in the room. On the outside, they may look calm, cool, and collected. Inside they wrestle with overthinking, shame spirals, and never-ending to-do lists. Over time, that internal pressure morphs into resentment—a mixing bowl of anger, envy, and judgment. Others seem far too lax about, well, everything.

Ones want to be good, but they'll settle for being right.

At their best, Ones relax their perfectionism and release resentment. Enneagram expert Chris Heuertz writes that they realize the "nuance between the binaries of right and wrong, good and bad, or perfection and imperfection." When Ones lower their shoulders and un-clench their jaws, they invite their natural power of creating order out of chaos. With flexibility, they become inspiring problem-solvers, empathetic motivators, and compassionate advocates for fairness and belonging. Ultimately, Ones remind us that true integrity shines brightest when we balance high standards with a willingness to let life (and ourselves) be delightfully imperfect.

Heart Group

Enneagram Two: The Considerate Giver

Trusted Tactic	Help
Fundamental Fear	Being rejected, dispensable, needy or unworthy
Driving Desire	To be needed and wanted
Persistent Pattern	Pride
Lasting Longing	You are wanted.
Feels individual emotions of others | Connector | Silver Lining	

Warm, welcoming, and always ready to lend a hand, Enneagram Twos thrive on genuine relationships, but they believe they have to earn love by helping others. Twos make themselves indispensable, jumping headfirst into helping before anyone even asks. In their eyes, helping guarantees their place in a relationship, dodging rejection and proving their worth. Trouble is, this easily slips into manipulation: "If I make myself indispensable, you couldn't possibly toss me aside." While Twos generally aren't scheming villains, they do need to watch out for that little voice urging them to do more, give more, and be more, just so they'll feel loved and secure in a relationship.

Surprisingly, the Two's persistent pattern of pride looks like humility personified ("Oh, it's no trouble at all. I'm happy to help!"). In reality, when Twos slip into toxic self-sacrifice, they deny their needs, convinced they exist above the realm of normal human requirements. They also have a knack for believing they know exactly what others need. This well-intentioned but presumptive approach leads to unsolicited advice and unnecessary activities. When others don't appreciate their efforts, the Two feels the very rejection they were trying to avoid by helping.

Twos want love, but they'll settle for appreciation.

At their best, Twos learn to identify "What is mine to do?" and set healthy boundaries. In this balanced state, Twos become empathetic mentors who foster genuine connection and develop the people around them. They still anticipate needs, but they don't assume everything falls to them, or that they have to sacrifice themselves to have significance. Twos show us all how to give fully to others and give the same love and acceptance to ourselves.

Enneagram Three: The Successful Inventor

Trusted Tactic	Achieve
Fundamental Fear	Failure or being worthless.
Driving Desire	Being valued
Persistent Pattern	Vainglory
Lasting Longing	You are worthy simply by being you.
Feels the emotions of the group | Trailblazer | Cool Cucumber	

Living, breathing motivational posters, Enneagram Threes crush the goal, seize the opportunity, and reinvent themselves for that next big win. Underneath the natural-winner façade, they're desperately trying to manage shame by proving their worth through efficiency and achievement. To add to the trouble, the achievement metrics are external, "Will this make me look good to others?" Whatever the environment demands, they'll adapt—often at lightning speed—to keep that curated "I'm killing it" image intact. And with every reinvention, they move further from their authentic selves.

This hustling for their worth costs the Three. Chasing the next goal is exhausting and requires suppressing those pesky emotions (Hey, feelings slow you down.). When a coworker's inefficiency blocks their path to success or fails to keep up, the shame-fueled frustration comes out swinging (emails at 3 a.m. or a polite-but-icy "I'll handle it myself").

Threes read the room, immediately sensing who's the most influential person in it. They rearrange themselves to fit what that group wants. Appearing to be the ideal go-getter, they lose track of who they really are beneath all the glittering achievements. Meanwhile, they might shame others who don't keep the pace, not understanding why everyone doesn't have to perform at 110%. Because anything less is unacceptable, and it's baffling that mediocrity could ever be okay. Yet deep down, they want to be able to give less effort and still be seen as valuable.

Threes want to be worthy without the work, but they'll settle for a chart of gold stars.

At their best, Threes rest in this fact: they are human beings, not human doings. They reconnect with their true, authentic identity and begin to define success for themselves, rather than chase empty glories that never satisfy. The compulsion to gather all the gold stars eases, and they accept that failure is a part of the process of winning. They also open that dusty box of emotions on the shelf and allow themselves (and others) a little extra space to feel. They still inspire us to achieve but no longer tie their worth to what they do. Threes show us that being what everyone else wants is a losing game and winning means accepting the limits of our ever-worthy humanity.

Enneagram Four: The Romantic Individualist

Trusted Tactic	Create
Fundamental Fear	Being insignificant, typical, or flawed. Lacking unique identity.
Driving Desire	Be authentically yourself
Persistent Pattern	Envy
Lasting Longing	You are seen for who you are.
Feels their emotions first | Professor | Dynamite	

Dwelling inside a rich internal landscape of feelings, beauty, and imagination, Enneagram Fours crave authenticity and long to be fully known. They fear they have a tragic flaw, a missing piece within them that others seem to possess—and own it with ease. Whether it's painting vivid canvases, penning heartfelt poetry, or simply cultivating an intangible atmosphere, Fours imbue life with depth and intensity. Behind the scenes, their creative expressions come from deep pain and melancholy, wondering if anyone sees them. Never wanting to be ordinary, they imagine an ideal that they can never quite reach while believing that other people can't really see their suffering or true selves. And everyone else seems to be able to enjoy it all so easily.

Fours despise small talk and welcome complexities and paradoxes. They are at once wistful and passionate, spontaneous yet reflective. And they lean in hard to that, amplifying their emotions as a way to feel truly alive, pulling friends into swirling seas of memories or imagination. Whatever the emotion, Fours want it more intense because that feels like the path to authenticity: not angry, but livid; not happy, elated; not sad, morose. But having feelings, then thoughts about the feelings, then more feelings about the thoughts about the feelings... leaves Fours stuck in cycles of longing rather than taking action. Both craving and shunning external validation, Fours often resist practical solutions that feel too "everyone does that."

Fours want to be known, but they'll settle for being noticed.

At their best, Enneagram Fours invite the world into authenticity, deep beauty, and powerful insights. When they recognize that they already are inherently special (no grand display required), they channel their capacity for beauty and authenticity into meaningful action. They bring us back to the values we say we want to live by, aligning actions to those ideals. Fours remind us how to be fully human, revealing the unique gifts in the most ordinary moments.

Head Group

Enneagram Five: The Curious Specialist

Trusted Tactic	Intellectualize
Fundamental Fear	Being incompetent, ignorant, or helpless
Driving Desire	To be capable and competent
Persistent Pattern	Avarice
Lasting Longing	Your needs are not a problem.
Internalizes Fear | Professor | Cool Cucumber	

Reserved, private, and curious, Enneagram Fives believe competence and capability will keep them safe from the insecurity of not knowing. If they can master the facts—researching, analyzing, and synthesizing every piece of data and related information—then maybe they'll stave off any threat of internal depletion. Believing it's not okay to be too comfortable, Fives see their own needs as an intellectual exercise in solving a research problem statement. Yet the constant inquiry, analysis, and questioning leave the Five with a significant amount of energy management. Think of a Five as starting each day at 60% battery, and they've got to work with that for the rest of the day. They work meticulously to preserve energy and avoid unwanted demands.

Fives often get stuck in planning mode, believing that once they've mapped out every possibility, they've effectively solved the problem. Oh but wait, they didn't actually take action to complete the plan. They can fall down a research rabbit hole (Reddit thread, data dive, library session), convinced they don't yet have enough information to make a decision. Meanwhile, their fear of depletion can lead to hoarding time, resources, and knowledge—a tendency known as avarice. Interaction with the outside world feels like it drains their internal battery even faster, so they keep to themselves to protect their mental reserves.

Fives want to be safe in the unknown, but they'll settle for being the competent expert.

At their best, Fives offer specialized expertise, bringing invaluable data, context, and institutional memory to everyone around them (and usually a witty comment that surprises everyone). They begin to balance curiosity and investigation with experimental, forward action, trusting they already have enough insight to act. Additionally, they believe asking for help doesn't equate to incompetence. Fives' careful observations and thorough thinking become indispensable assets for teams and projects. Ultimately, Fives remind the world that curiosity navigates us all safely through the mysteries of living.

Enneagram Six: The Loyal Skeptic

Trusted Tactic	Prepare
Fundamental Fear	To lack support or guidance, being blamed or abandoned
Driving Desire	To be secure and have guidance and support
Persistent Pattern	Angst
Lasting Longing	You are safe.
Externalizes Fear | Connector | Dynamite	

Questioning and preparing, Enneagram Sixes live in a world of potential pitfalls, ever on guard for what might go wrong. Afraid they'll be blamed or abandoned, they prepare for every eventuality for themselves and others as if they were writing the worst-case scenario guidebook. Sixes have more than one internal critical voice. They have an internal conference room hosting a committee of competing voices: "Have we considered this angle? What if that happens? Are we sure we can trust this person?" Ever made decisions by committee? Exhausting. All the internal debate erodes trust in their ability to make decisions in the face of a world that feels extremely insecure. Hence, they prepare for it all.

Sixes flow along a continuum—in Enneagram literature, it's called phobic and counterphobic. But here's what that means: Some Sixes lean toward compliance and rule-following, while others run to oppositional scrutiny against authority. Constantly testing whether leaders and systems are actually worthy of their loyalty, individual Sixes seesaw on the continuum depending on the committee report.

The elaborate scenario building is simply overthinking that leads to indecision, self-doubt, and the constant companion of low-grade angst. Because Sixes crave security and reassurance, they second-guess themselves and others, worried someone's overlooking a crucial detail. To manage the fear, they barrage others with questions, unintentionally appearing resistant or parental. Frequently, the truth is they want to ensure they've poked enough holes to help an idea succeed.

Sixes want security, but they'll settle for being the ever-ready supporter.

At their best, Sixes transform "what-if" worries into pragmatic plans. Because nobody sees the hidden snags and potential crises like a Six, their questions spot risks, leading to robust strategies. They bring people together through genuine concern, using their talent for collective problem-solving to spot risks and craft robust strategies. When they trust their own judgment (and tell the internal committee to sit it on down), they discover they may not be fearless, but they can trust themselves. Rather than letting fear rule the day, healthy Sixes balance trusting the community with courage to have faith in their abilities. In an unpredictable world, Sixes remind us that solid plans (and maybe a few backup plans) go a long way, and courage means feeling the fear and doing it anyway.

Enneagram Seven: The Enthusiastic Visionary

Trusted Tactic	Reframe
Fundamental Fear	Experiencing pain. To feel trapped or limited.
Driving Desire	To be fully content and satisfied
Persistent Pattern	Voracity
Lasting Longing	You will be taken care of.
Ignores Fear | Trailblazer | Silver Lining	

Excitable, future-oriented, and deeply optimistic, Enneagram Sevens strive to find the next thing that will satisfy the internal discontentment they keep hidden. Beneath brainstorming options and finding the silver side of that raincloud, Sevens desperately want to evade pain at all costs. Because their Seven nature tells them others won't come through for them, they've learned to find multiple options (including an escape hatch), to keep themselves safe. While others see days filled with group chats, airplane tickets, creative endeavors, and the latest innovation, Sevens are actually managing a deep fear of missing out, being trapped in disappointment, or—heaven forbid—not reframing but actually facing the low-level anxiety creeping around in the basement of their minds.

Sevens want enduring contentment, but they'll settle for thrills.

Because limitations, micromanagement, or even boredom feel like pain, Sevens keep themselves preoccupied with various pursuits—both mentally and in the real world. They're often switch-tasking, reading multiple books at once, juggling disparate projects, or even talking about where they could go on the next vacation while wading in the ocean on their current trip. If all else fails, Sevens simply grab for "Well, at least..." or "It's not a crisis—it's an adventure!" Without awareness, reframing mushrooms into toxic positivity, leaving others confused, hurt, and exhausted. FOMO might be the Seven's motivator, but ironically, the bigger fear is being left alone to deal with those messy feelings they've been sidestepping with all that fun.

At their best, Sevens lead with hopeful vision, bringing joy and deep empathy with them. They're masters of turning challenges into opportunities and sparking creative solutions that others miss. When they learn it's okay to not be okay (and don't have others always expecting them to be their personal mood booster), they begin to trust that life won't implode if they pause long enough to feel those uncomfortable emotions. Their natural optimism matures into genuine resilience, and they surprise people with their depth and commitment.

Sevens remind all of us that while we have endless imagination, limits are good. We don't have to jam every waking minute with novelty to feel safe.

Appendix B:
Fillable Frameworks

These pages are designed to help you apply the Joyosity™ practices directly in your life.

- Make copies for your own personal use—to keep, redo, or reflect on over time.
- Visit jennwhitmer.com/playbook-tools to download PDFs and find other tools like the breath videos, Play Persona Quiz, or the Personal Board Journal templates.

Using the frameworks, AKA What's ok and what's not ok: I love when people use and talk about these tools—that's what they're for! You're welcome to make copies for yourself as often as you need or show a friend, coach, or colleague how you've used a framework in your own growth.

To keep this work sustainable, please don't share or distribute the actual files or templates themselves or make copies for your whole team or group without written permission.

Johari Window

	Known to Self	Hidden from Self
Known to Others	Open	Blind Spot
Hidden from Others	Façade	Unknown

Johari Window

Values List

Abundance	Acceptance	Accessibility	Accomplishment
Accountability	Accuracy	Achievement	Acknowledgement
Activeness	Adaptability	Adoration	Adroitness
Advancement	Adventure	Affection	Affluence
Aggressiveness	Agility	Alertness	Altruism
Amazement	Ambition	Amusement	Anticipation
Appreciation	Approachability	Approval	Art
Articulacy	Artistry	Assertiveness	Assurance
Attentiveness	Attractiveness	Audacity	Availability
Awareness	Awe	Balance	Beauty
Being the best	Belonging	Benevolence	Bliss
Boldness	Bravery	Brilliance	Buoyancy
Calmness	Camaraderie	Candor	Capability
Care	Carefulness	Celebrity	Certainty
Challenge	Change	Charity	Charm
Chastity	Cheerfulness	Clarity	Cleanliness
Clear mindedness	Cleverness	Closeness	Comfort
Commitment	Community	Compassion	Competence
Competition	Completion	Composure	Concentration
Confidence	Conformity	Congruency	Connection
Consciousness	Conservation	Consistency	Contentment
Continuity	Contribution	Control	Conviction
Conviviality	Coolness	Cooperation	Cordiality
Correctness	Country	Courage	Courtesy
Craftiness	Creativity	Credibility	Cunning
Curiosity	Daring	Decisiveness	Decorum
Deference	Delight	Dependability	Depth
Desire	Determination	Devotion	Devoutness
Dexterity	Dignity	Diligence	Direction
Directness	Discipline	Discovery	Discretion
Diversity	Dominance	Dreaming	Drive
Duty	Dynamism	Eagerness	Ease
Economy	Ecstasy	Education	Effectiveness
Efficiency	Elation	Elegance	Empathy
Encouragement	Endurance	Energy	Enjoyment
Entertainment	Enthusiasm	Environmentalism	Ethics
Euphoria	Excellence	Excitement	Exhilaration
Expectancy	Expediency	Experience	Expertise
Exploration	Expressiveness	Extravagance	Extroversion

Exuberance	Fairness	Faith	Fame
Family	Fascination	Fashion	Fearlessness
Ferocity	Fidelity	Fierceness	Financial independence
Firmness	Fitness	Flexibility	Flow
Fluency	Focus	Fortitude	Frankness
Freedom	Friendliness	Friendship	Frugality
Fun	Gallantry	Generosity	Gentility
Giving	Grace	Gratitude	Gregariousness
Growth	Guidance	Happiness	Harmony
Health	Heart	Helpfulness	Heroism
Holiness	Honesty	Honor	Hopefulness
Hospitality	Humility	Humor	Hygiene
Imagination	Impact	Impartiality	Independence
Individuality	Industry	Influence	Ingenuity
Inquisitiveness	Insightfulness	Inspiration	Integrity
Intellect	Intelligence	Intensity	Intimacy
Intrepidness	Introspection	Introversion	Intuition
Intuitiveness	Inventiveness	Investing	Involvement
Joy	Judiciousness	Justice	Keenness
Kindness	Knowledge	Leadership	Learning
Liberation	Liberty	Lightness	Liveliness
Logic	Longevity	Love	Loyalty
Majesty	Making a difference	Marriage	Mastery
Maturity	Meaning	Meekness	Mellowness
Meticulousness	Mindfulness	Modesty	Motivation
Mysteriousness	Nature	Neatness	Nerve
Nonconformity	Obedience	Open-mindedness	Openness
Optimism	Order	Organization	Originality
Outdoors	Outlandishness	Outrageousness	Partnership
Patience	Passion	Peace	Perceptiveness
Perfection	Perkiness	Perseverance	Persistence
Persuasiveness	Philanthropy	Piety	Playfulness
Pleasantness	Pleasure	Poise	Popularity
Potency	Power	Practicality	Pragmatism
Precision	Preparedness	Presence	Pride
Privacy	Proactivity	Professionalism	Prosperity
Prudence	Punctuality	Purity	Rationality
Realism	Reason	Reasonableness	Recognition
Recreation	Refinement	Reflection	Relaxation
Reliability	Relief	Religiousness	Reputation

Resilience	Resolution	Resolve	Resourcefulness
Respect	Responsibility	Rest	Restraint
Reverence	Richness	Rigor	Sacredness
Sacrifice	Sagacity	Saintliness	Sanguinity
Satisfaction	Science	Security	Self-control
Selflessness	Self-reliance	Self-respect	Sensitivity
Sensuality	Serenity	Service	Sexiness
Sexuality	Sharing	Shrewdness	Significance
Silence	Silliness	Simplicity	Sincerity
Skillfulness	Solidarity	Solitude	Sophistication
Soundness	Speed	Spirit	Spirituality
Spontaneity	Spunk	Stability	Status
Stealth	Stillness	Strength	Structure
Success	Support	Supremacy	Surprise
Sympathy	Synergy	Teaching	Teamwork
Temperance	Thankfulness	Thoroughness	Thoughtfulness
Thrift	Tidiness	Timeliness	Traditionalism
Tranquility	Transcendence	Trust	Trustworthiness
Truth	Understanding	Unflappability	Uniqueness
Unity	Usefulness	Utility	Valor
Variety	Victory	Vigor	Virtue
Vision	Vitality	Vivacity	Volunteering
Warmheartedness	Warmth	Watchfulness	Wealth
Wholeheartedness	Willfulness	Willingness	Winning
Wisdom	Wittiness	Wonder	Worthiness
Youthfulness	Zeal		

Values: Identifying Meaning and Attaching Experiences

Value: Definition:		
Aligned Actions	**Misaligned Actions**	**Situations & Stories**

Shift the Script

Sustaining Story:	
Times when this story was true.	What happened? How did I feel?
Imagine for a moment this story is always true. How would you show up differently? What actions will you take?	

Clear (Paint Done and TASC)

Paint Done:
T: Who owns the task?
A: Do they have authority?
S: Are they set up for success?
C: Is there a checklist?

Absorbing Stories (Story Frame)

Character	Emotions	Moment	Details

Before	POP	Now

I Statements

Sentence Starter	Content
I feel...	Emotion
When you do/don't do/this happens...	Specific situation
Because I think it means...	Why you care, the story you're telling yourself
I'd like...	What you want
Would you consider...	Specific Action

Board Brainstorm

MENTORS	
Name:	Challenger · Cheerleader · Connector
Name:	Challenger · Cheerleader · Connector
Name:	Challenger · Cheerleader · Connector
Name:	Challenger · Cheerleader · Connector
Name:	Challenger · Cheerleader · Connector
Guiding Voice:	Challenger · Cheerleader · Connector

SPONSORS	
Name:	Challenger · Cheerleader · Connector
Name:	Challenger · Cheerleader · Connector
Name:	Challenger · Cheerleader · Connector
Name:	Challenger · Cheerleader · Connector
Name:	Challenger · Cheerleader · Connector
Guiding Voice:	Challenger · Cheerleader · Connector

COACHES	
Name:	Challenger · Cheerleader · Connector
Name:	Challenger · Cheerleader · Connector
Name:	Challenger · Cheerleader · Connector
Name:	Challenger · Cheerleader · Connector
Name:	Challenger · Cheerleader · Connector
Guiding Voice:	Challenger · Cheerleader · Connector

PEERS	
Name:	Challenger · Cheerleader · Connector
Name:	Challenger · Cheerleader · Connector
Name:	Challenger · Cheerleader · Connector
Name:	Challenger · Cheerleader · Connector
Name:	Challenger · Cheerleader · Connector
Guiding Voice:	Challenger · Cheerleader · Connector

Board Assembly

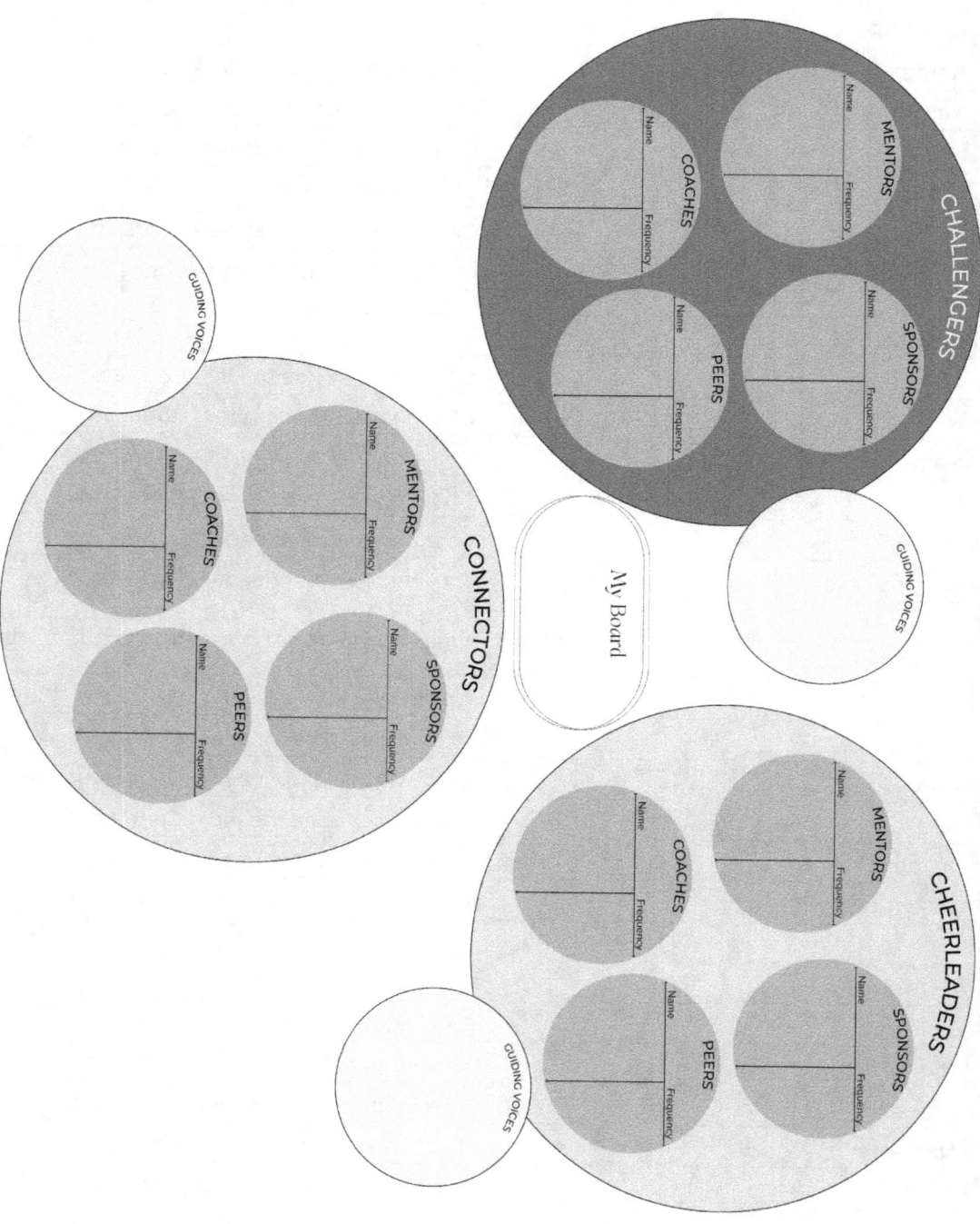

Personal Board Journal

Fill in your board here or use Google or Notion template in the online resources.

Name	Contact Info	Role	Support Style	Reasons Selected	Connection Frequency	Notes

Decision Insight Decoder

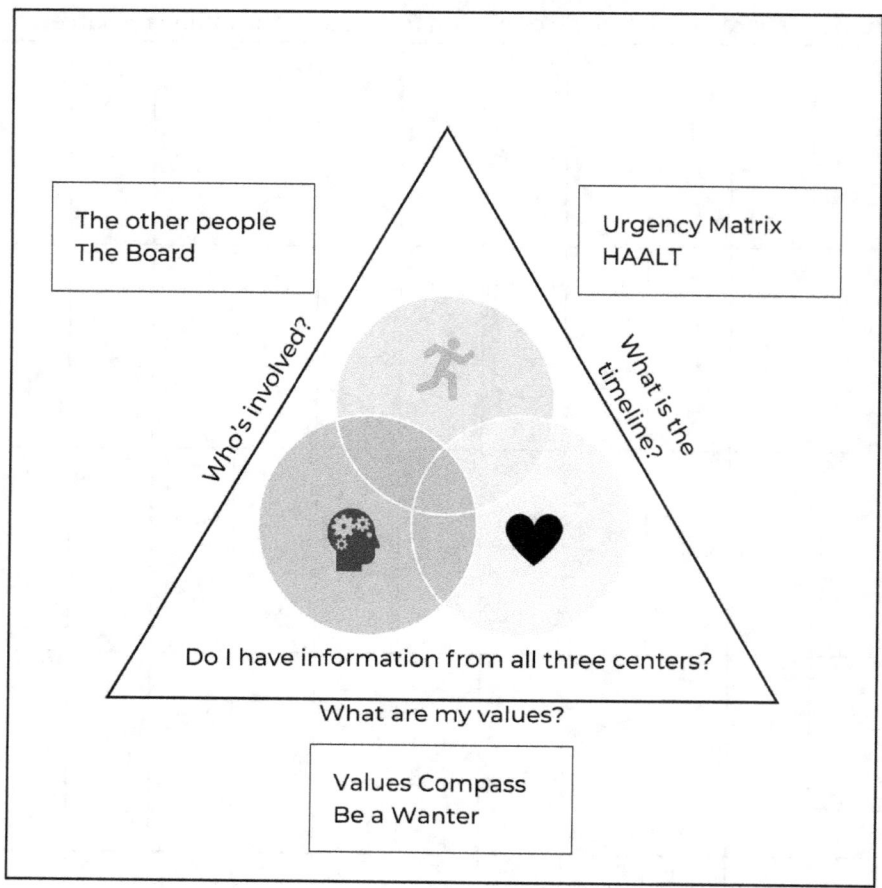

The other people
The Board

Urgency Matrix
HAALT

Who's involved?

What is the timeline?

Do I have information from all three centers?

What are my values?

Values Compass
Be a Wanter

Manager Week

Time	Mon	Tue	Wed	Thurs	Fri	Sat	Sun
6:00 am							
6:30 am							
7:00 am							
7:30 am							
8:00 am							
8:30 am							
9:00 am							
9:30 am							
10:00 am							
10:30 am							
11:00 am							
11:30 am							
12:00 am							
12:30 am							
1:00 pm							
1:30 pm							
2:00 pm							
2:30 pm							
3:00 pm							
3:30 pm							
4:00 pm							
4:30 pm							
5:00 pm							
5:30 pm							
6:00 pm							
6:30 pm							
7:00 pm							
7:30 pm							
8:00 pm							
8:30 pm							
9:00 pm							
9:30 pm							

Maker Week

Time	Mon	Tue	Wed	Thurs	Fri	Sat	Sun
Start Time							
Morning							
Midday							
Afternoon							
Evening							
End time							

Musician Week

Time	Mon	Tues	Wed	Thurs	Fri	Sat	Sun
Start Time							
Work Time and Type of Day							
After Work							
End Time							

Your Next Play: Work with Jenn

I can help you walk through these plays to uncover what's blocking your joy and guide you to build systems that work for you—not against you. Let's talk about options for one-on-one coaching, small group experiences, or interactive team sessions that spark connection, clarity, and lasting change.

From individual 30-minutes breakthrough sessions to a keynote for your entire organization, there's a way to bring Joyosity™ to every level of your leadership and culture.

- Individual or Group Coaching: jennwhitmer.com/coaching
- Speaking or working with your team: jennwhitmer.com/speaking
- Not sure where to start? Head to jennwhitmer.com/contact send us a message.

Jenn Whitmer,
Your Coach and Joy Strategist

Jenn Whitmer helps leaders with Joyosity, creating positive culture with complex people. Through solving conflict, cultivating communication, and celebrating each person's uniqueness, she helps teams work better together—and actually enjoy it.

An international keynote and TEDx speaker, Enneagram specialist, and former educator, Jenn brings research, laughter, and real-world experience to every room.

Now, through her talks, coaching, *Joyosity* Podcast, and with her book *Joyosity: How to Cultivate Intense Happiness in Work & Life (Even If Things Are What They Are)*, she helps organizations retain employees, increase efficiency, and create workplaces that are people-first, purpose-driven, and clearly full of joy.

When she's not helping leaders, she's probably breezing through TSA PreCheck with her Frownies on, wishing life were a musical (Newsies, obviously), and quoting *Ted Lasso* gems like, "Don't you dare settle for fine." Jenn lives in St. Louis, Missouri, with her husband, Michael, their four kids, and a judgmental Russian Blue cat.